THE PURPLE BOOK OF CAREER STRATEGIES

EXPLORING OPTIONS AND OPPORTUNITIES

D1445366

GARTH TOOMBS

The Purple Book of Career Strategies
Copyright © 2001 by Garth Toombs & Associates Inc.
Member of Verity Filion Inc.
Lee Hecht Harrison, Global Partner
Previous Editions 1994, 1997.

This book presents the author's opinions. The author does not intend to render legal or other professional service by presenting these opinions. The author and publisher specifically disclaim responsibility for loss or risk incurred as a consequence of the application of any advice or information presented here.

Requests for permission to make copies of any part of the work should be mailed to:
Garth Toombs & Associates Inc., #1000, 500 – 4th Avenue SW, Calgary, Alberta T2P 2V6 Canada, or

Garth Toombs & Associates (Edmonton) Inc., 1207, 10104 – 103 Avenue, Edmonton, Alberta T5J 0H8 Canada

All exercises, instruments, tables, and diagrams used here are the property of Garth Toombs & Associates Inc.

Toombs, Garth, 1935 –
        The Purple Book of Career Strategies: Exploring Options and Opportunities
                1. Career Development   2. Job Search Techniques
ISBN 0-9698879-3-0

Cover design and illustrations by Dean Stanton
Printed in Canada by Style-Craft Printing Ltd.

Table of Contents

INTRODUCTION

What kinds of employed people do we see each day? I start my day by watching a couple of television personalities report on the morning news. I get in my car, and except for people in other cars, I don't run into any employed people until I greet the security guard in the office building. Sometimes I go to the second floor for my breakfast where I am in touch with a cook and another food service person who takes my money. Of course, in the office I see all of the counselors and administrators of our firm. Also, I am on good terms with the office delivery person who brings up our mail and am on nodding terms with the cleaning people, many of whom don't speak English very well. There are phone calls from human resource professionals, managers of various types, and people whose backgrounds are in engineering, business, law, accounting and marketing. If I go out at noon, I run into many professional people and support people who work in the nearby buildings. I also see the shoe-shine people and many more food service people at the local food fairs. In the afternoon, on the way home, I may stop for gas and talk briefly with the clerk in the gas kiosk. Over the course of a week or two I run into many more store clerks, a barber, all the fitness and other staff at the YMCA, the staff at the bank, and my business and professional friends at the Rotary Club.

This is just the tip of the iceberg in terms of the great variety and diversity of employed people.

What is the experience of being employed? Is it just to have a job? Are we all in transition in life from job to job, always looking to improve our lot? What opportunities are there to improve, develop our skills, and get higher pay?

Being employed is very important to most of us. Our livelihood depends on employment. The view we have of our worth and competence comes from work experiences. It uses up massive amounts of our time. On the job, we improve and increase our technical skills and we learn how to work more effectively with others. Many of us are proud of our work achievements and look for how we can leverage them to get a better position either in our organization or in some other. Clearly a person's career is of great importance to him or her. Yet it is constantly threatened.

The threats to working life come from a number of places.

Job stresses, over-work, conflict with co-workers, constant change and over-learned tasks take their toll on us. The workplace can be the source of a great deal of unhappiness.

Management is often not even conscious of the needs of the staff. People stagnate in jobs they can easily do. Management does not give leadership to overcome destructive internal competition and to assist people seriously burned-out from stress and over-work. There are unresolved communication problems, inconsistent discipline, inadequate systems and inefficient ways of doing work. Often, people down in the ranks of the organization know exactly what it would take to improve the organization on many fronts, but they are never asked, or their interest in helping is dismissed.

In the world of work, major changes are taking place in almost every area of endeavor. We know that many jobs are being eliminated. The people affected must move on, learn new skills and adapt. This can be a good thing. Stimulation and growth come from the constant challenge to do what we could not do before. Many people conclude that they are not a good fit for a large organization, or for any type of traditionally based work. They may try to start their own business, or do something totally out of the ordinary, such as a friend of mine who consults on public relations a few days a week in Vancouver, when she is not gardening and relaxing at her new home on a small island off Vancouver Island.

Many of us experience multiple careers during a working life. Fewer people work for large organizations. We must become more self-reliant as organizations play a smaller role in ensuring our lifetime security.

There is little comfort in this for the person who needs to find work or in some way create an opportunity to earn income. This is particularly true for the army of people whose jobs or skills have become redundant in our fast-changing world. Today the world needs experts at using computers and other high tech and specialized equipment. Workers everywhere require knowledge of new methods. Many must be more effective in interpersonal relationships as more and more jobs require cooperative effort, interfacing with customers or negotiating contracts. People also need to be motivated and energized to make the necessary contacts leading to new opportunities.

The career strategy for the future requires one to be interdependent, responsive to change, always learning, understanding of the pressures placed on us by our chaotic world and effective in relating to other people. This is quite a departure from the expectations of stability and security of the past.

This book provides a framework for considering your career and offers advice on what to do when career change becomes necessary. It provides many ideas, suggestions, tips and tactics to help you consider your stage in life, your career or vocation, how to job search, and entrepreneurship. There are chapters on the traditional concerns of resumé preparation, interviewing and networking. There are also sections to stimulate thought on making choices, emotional makeup and how your personality impacts on the ability to affect a change in your career.

Each of us will, in the final analysis, "do what we will do" to seek out new opportunities. Our personality and style impacts all the things we do, including career planning and opportunity searching. There is no one magic career strategy. There are many routes leading to successful re-employment or to new life opportunities.

This is the third edition of this book. It started, in its first edition, as a compilation of articles written for a monthly newsletter. The second edition added new sections on career planning, technology and entrepreneurship. This edition has been extensively re-written and several new areas have been added. Also, advice changes with the changing times, and we are conscious of continually researching, identifying new techniques and new approaches to assist people through career changes.

Many people have helped in the production of this edition. Dean Stanton provided illustrations giving a new dimension to the content. Ann Toombs made valuable content and editing suggestions. Kathy Richardier, who often provides us with editing assistance, looked at every page and made improvements to the book's overall readability. Many members of the staff of Garth Toombs and Associates Inc. provided advice on how to improve the book. A special thanks to Susan Komhyr who played a role in setting up the content and cleaning up some obvious problems. We also appreciated help and advice from Jackie Brooks, Ivan Cancik, Diane Cunningham, Sonja Henning, Len Lavoie, Janice Levesque, Laurie Maslak, Laraine McIntyre and Danielle Timmons. Thanks also to Ken Scott who provided content on entrepreneurship in the 2nd Edition, much of which has been incorporated in this revision. We are especially indebted to the job search work teams of clients of the firm who generated questions about the career and job search process. Many of these questions, with answers, appear at the end of the various Chapters. We are also indebted to the owners of the firm, Ross Gilker, Tracey Lillis and Mark Toombs, who also provided input on content and gave the necessary support to ensure this project would be completed.

Garth Toombs

PLANNING: INITIAL CONSIDERATIONS

WHERE WILL I GO NEXT?

Our work lives ought to be in constant flux. We should be moving on, taking on increasingly more complex and demanding tasks. If we stay in the same job too long, we will know the job well, but we will become personally stale. Unless we can add new elements to the job, or it provides opportunities for special project work, we risk spending months or years in the wishy-washy world of job complacency.

Some people see this happening in their own lives and take action.

Joel worked for the recreation department of a medium sized city. He had held various positions. Then he got an assignment to run a youth drop-in centre for the troubled young people in a poorer working class area of the city. At first, it was very challenging. With much to learn and a busy schedule, he found himself totally absorbed most days and evenings of the week. With the unpredictable behaviour of his clients, he faced many crises. He particularly concentrated on teaching group problem-solving and setting behavioural limits.

About a year into the job, Joel realized that his satisfaction level was dropping. He saw the same problems occur again and again. He always felt good when he effectively dealt with the problems presented by new kids arriving in the centre, but he could see that he had peaked using his current skills.

Joel went to his supervisor, the Manager of Youth Programs about a transfer, or new opportunity. The Manager was sympathetic, but had little to offer Joel. Everyone was pleased with his work, and in particular, his innovative approach in working in this difficult area. The Manager told him that everyone hoped he would stay.

But Joel knew he needed to move on. He had learned the work and developed many new skills in youth leadership. He had been as successful as any of his predecessors. Now, he wanted to find a new challenge to continue to test his abilities in youth leadership.

Two years after he had started at the drop-in centre he found a new position in an allied, but very different field, as the manager of a youth recreation complex. He was energized by the prospects of this new opportunity, yet sad to leave an area for which he had developed a real affection, even though he had come to the point where it was no longer challenging.

We see this story repeated again and again. We all need to challenge ourselves with more responsibility, different things to do, and more complex work.

For some of us this choice is taken from us as the organization we work for changes its focus and carries out a downsizing, choosing us to leave. Often organizations do us a big favor. We have been unable to make the move ourselves to find more complex work, and the organization forces our hand.

STEPS IN A JOB SEARCH

People ask, "What steps do I need to take to get another job?" These steps are different for everyone, since each of us has a unique personality and a different life plan. The following nine steps can be a starting point for a constructive approach. Most of the steps are covered in one or more sections of this book.

1.   *Come to terms with leaving your present employment.*

You may be planning to leave your present position, or you could be released. When you finally leave, some degree of emotional turmoil will result. Don't deny those feelings! Understand what you are going through and allow yourself the time to live with your emotions and return to normal. Once you are in a new situation, your day-to-day attention to your new activities will help you get over any residual grief you have about leaving your former employer.

2.   *Get your finances in order.*

Financial planning is important at every point in life. When you contemplate leaving your job, it becomes even more important. Have you taken into account all the changes to your financial situation? Will your new salary be higher or lower? Will you have as many perks as you now have? What are the long-term implications from a financial perspective?

If you have been released and are given a financial package, there are a number of cash flow and tax issues to consider. Planning to buy a business, moving into a lower paying position, or being out of work for an extended period have financial implications. Seek the advice of an independent financial or tax consultant.

3.   Decide what you want to do.

Some people find this very easy. They have had a plan in place for some time, or they simply expect to move on to another position in the same field. Others need to go through a systematic process of looking at their interests, aptitudes, skills and values. Read Chapter 2 on Planning Your Career – And Your Life.

4.   Prepare for the search.

Prepare a resumé. Get ready to respond to ads, talk to recruiters and start your networking campaign. Know how to answer the difficult question about why you want to leave, or have left, your previous job. Go over possible questions you will be asked as you contact people or go to interviews. See Chapters 5, 6 and 7.

5.   Get references in place.

Meet with potential references to talk about your career aspirations. Leave a resumé, or a profile sheet, and a business card. Discuss the handling of reference calls. Since letters of reference don't have the same credibility as references provided by voice, put an emphasis on finding referees willing to respond to phone calls about you. Chapter 8 deals with references.

6.   Set out a priority plan.

If you are planning to leave a job, or if you have been released, you need a daily, weekly and monthly plan for conducting your job search. Place the emphasis on meeting new people every day, if

Iceberg Concept

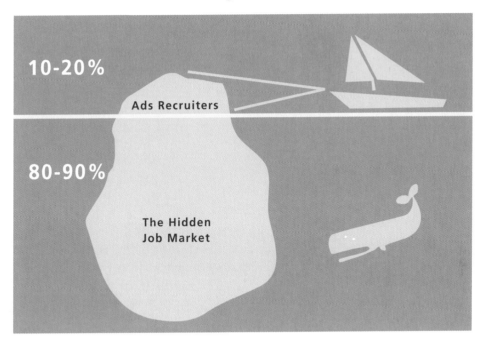

10-20%

Ads Recruiters

80-90%

**The Hidden
Job Market**

possible, by telephone – people with whom you can seek personal networking interviews. Respond every day to relevant advertisements. Write thank-you notes to people you have met and spoken with who have given you good advice. Check out career opportunities that appear on web sites. Read Chapter 4 on The Job Search Schedule.

7.   *Carry out research on prospects.*

You do this as your search proceeds. Directories, newspapers, professional journals, the Internet and other sources can all be used to find out about organizations that might employ you. Be well informed about the marketplace. Understand the businesses of prospective employers before you meet with them.

8.   *Prepare for interviews very carefully.*

Go over possible interview questions, and ask your spouse or a friend to "interview" you ahead of time. Consider how you will dress. Arrive five minutes before the scheduled interview.

Remember that a positive, enthusiastic and upbeat approach can be the key not only to success in an interview but also to developing and maintaining contacts in your quest for your future place of employment. Chapter 7 goes into detail on the interviewing process.

9.   *Keep up a constant pace of work.*

Success at a job or opportunity search usually results from a sustained daily schedule of directed activities. You must take the initiative. Discuss your circumstances with people you know and with people you don't know. This book will help you with these and other aspects of the opportunity search process.

QUESTIONS AND ANSWERS

- *What is more important: taking the time to be well prepared to job search, or simply "getting out there," networking and applying for jobs?*

Both these elements are extremely important, but in the final analysis a successful job search is the result of much contacting and interviewing. If it were necessary to partially sacrifice one for the other, it would be better to do less preparation and more face-to-face contacting.

- *Is there some "trick" to getting yourself excited about searching for a job?*

Think of preparing for, and then going on a long journey to a far-away land. You need to plan and to know your destination. But finally, when you are on the journey, you must take the initiative to survive, to enjoy, to see what you want to see. Many times you will talk to strangers. Sometimes they will point you in the wrong direction, or give you inaccurate information, or even refuse to help. But if you keep asking, eventually you will get there.

That's about as "tricky" as a job search gets!

2

PLANNING YOUR CAREER — AND YOUR LIFE

We live in an increasingly complex world. At times, we wince at what appear to be impossible burdens and expectations. We despair both at the complexity of our jobs and at the boredom they eventually cause. There always seems to be something missing. We find ourselves thinking, "If I were leading a truly fulfilling, enjoyable, growth-oriented existence I would be doing more of ... I would be completely engrossed in ... I would have made a 180° turn to do ..."

Life is much more than a job or career. We have a variety of relationships of importance to us, both at work and away from work. We have interests and hobbies; we have skills we like to use. Considerable pain accompanies life for most people. We regret not having taken a particular course or degree. We regret not following through on a developing relationship. Images of past hurts, put-downs and failures nag at us, and at times we can't seem to get them out of our minds.

Planning your career is far from straightforward. Because of all the stresses and ambiguities of life, we tend to drift, picking up on opportunities as they arise. Some people move ahead in their careers on this basis, without much planning. Others find that a lack of planning produces fewer favourable results and they end up in careers which are not right for them, or they stay in jobs much longer than they should.

SELF-ASSESSMENT IN CAREER PLANNING

Self-assessment is a dynamic process. It doesn't start and stop at certain points in our lives. On the contrary, we must rethink over and over again where we have been, where we are now and where we would like to be going.

Most of us continually consider and reconsider our careers. About once every five years, we approach a turning point and attempt to make changes. For some, the change may represent only a minor adjustment to their present work situation. Others will make a major shift by changing jobs and adjusting other facets of their lives.

We change because of self-discovery, self-knowledge and greater maturity. Through an assessment process, we can systematically follow through with our plans for personal growth and change.

THE BUILDING BLOCKS TO PLANNING YOUR CAREER

There are 6 issue areas, or building blocks, in planning a career. Taking all of them into consideration gives us a better chance of making a rational decision about our future. Unfortunately, career planning, like all personal planning and thinking has a heavy element of "emotion" mixed up with it. We make sudden decisions without careful thought because of critical incidents in our lives. Or, we make a lasting career decision simply because of the good feeling we have that someone wants us for a particular job. It has nothing to do with our interests, aptitudes or long-term plans. Later in life, many people get into an "if only'" struggle with themselves. "If only" – I had stayed in school longer; "if only" I had agreed to that international assignment, "if only" I had used my talent for languages, and so on.

There will always be strong elements of irrationality and emotion in any decision about one's career. Some people call it "intuition" and make important decisions because they just feel they are the right ones to make. But, supporting quickly made plans with a thorough rational review certainly can't hurt.

Here are the <u>6 building blocks</u> to consider in moving towards a thoughtful decision about your career. They will be explained in detail in this Chapter.

<u>Building Block 1</u>. Your past, including your skills, achievements, past positions, natural abilities, education.

<u>Building Block 2</u>. Your future including your aspirations, dreams, plans, ideals.

<u>Building Block 3</u>. Who you are – values, motivation, purpose.

<u>Building Block 4</u>. Who you are – stress, health, response to change.

<u>Building Block 5</u>. Today's work reality – are there positions for you?

<u>Building Block 6</u>. Tomorrow's work reality – what does the long term future hold?

Building Block 1. Your Past

Each of us is anchored in what we have learned or acquired from past experience. We are unique and the product of various aptitudes and other characteristics inherited from our parents, learned from others or acquired on our own.

Skills

We have developed certain skills. Some require technical ability, some require us to use many parts of our body, others relate to how we talk or listen or persuade, and still others allow us to consider situations very broadly, or to be very narrow and specific. Very often we don't realize the extent of our skills and abilities until we very carefully consider them.   They fall into many categories:

Artistic

Physical – as in athletics

Social and helpful

Manual Dexterity

Technical – as in computer skills

Leadership – as in directing, managing, initiating, achieving consensus

Numerical – as in computation, accounting, statistics

Self-management – as in personal decision-making, being friendly

Selling – as in being persuasive

Thinking – as in researching, analyzing, conceptualizing, prioritizing

Word use – as in reading, writing, editing, speaking clearly

You can systematically determine your skill areas. They can also be matched with your interests. Taking a test, such as the **Strong Inventory**[1] will help you realize that you have many skills and

---

[1] Strong Interest Inventory, Strong, E.K. Jr., J.C. Hansen, D.P. Campbell. Consulting Psychology Press, Inc., 1985. It is a paper and pencil multiple-choice questionnaire that has proven valuable in assisting people to systematically identify their strongest interests.

abilities and a multitude of directions you can explore. However, for now, review the list above. Do any of these spring out at you, as areas of major skills or abilities? If up to three do, you probably are well tuned into your abilities. If most of them do, this may indicate that you have not differentiated your understanding of your skills.

You may have skills in each of these areas, but in which do you really shine? If you can't seem to choose any, or only one, it is likely because of lack of self-knowledge. Tests or questionnaires can be very helpful in creating an awareness of your ability areas.

Natural Attributes

We might also consider our natural ways of doing things. Some people believe we are born with natural tendencies. If we can take advantage of them, rather than constantly fighting them, we will lead happier and more fulfilling lives.

They fall into four categories.[2]

> **Idea People** – people who have a dominant natural ability in this area tend to be innovators and idea generators. They are spontaneous and do their work in the order of importance as it occurs to them. In meetings they are often the people coming up with one idea or solution after another.
>
> People who don't have natural tendencies in this area will likely consider idea people to be too fast off the mark with ideas and not organized enough.
>
> **Researcher** – A dominant natural ability in this area causes people to read, investigate and study. They are likely to be

---

[2] The Conative Connection, Kolbe, Kathy. Addison-Wesley Publishing Company, Inc., 1990. Ms. Kolbe actually referred to these four areas by the names, "Quick Start", "Fact Finder", "Follow Through", and "Implementer".

critical of those who don't dig deeply enough into subjects of importance. They will want to be sure of the "facts" before engaging in an important discussion with a group of people.

Those without this natural tendency can be observed skimming material, reading only the summary, and generally not digging deeply even into those subjects where they have an interest. They disliked school because they were expected to study things in depth. They typically did what they had to do to get the grades they wanted to get.

Methodical People – Those with this characteristic as a dominant natural ability, will do things in a well-organized way. They will make lists and check things off. The day and the week will be planned. Their office and desk will be orderly with everything in its place.

The opposite people are often messy and don't appear to others to be well organized, even though they may get all the necessary work done. They typically are not good at following things through to completion. They are poor at routine. Being forced to be organized makes them tense, as this does not come naturally to them.

Physical Person – Some people have a dominant tendency, seemingly from the day they were born, to relate well to things in the physical world and to use their bodies in the course of their daily activities. These are people who work with their hands (carpenters, surgeons) and who are naturally good at using different tools and equipment. They may also be easily adaptable to physical activities in sports or outdoor activities.

Of course, some people are the opposite, and don't do

physical things unless they absolutely have to, because their makeup is one that resists fixing and hammering.

Almost everyone has some of each of these tendencies: **Idea Person, Researcher, Methodical Person and Physical Person**. However, most of us will have strength in one particular area over the other three. There may also be one in which we are resistant; that is, we are the opposite of what is described.

If we can find employment where we can "be ourselves'" in terms of our natural dominant tendency or strength, we will work much more effectively.

These natural attributes have nothing to do with intelligence. Many people spend a lifetime working in areas they don't enjoy and in which they don't have a natural strength. A student can force herself to do research even though she may be a resistant researcher, in order to achieve her goal of the completion of the course. You can be sure, however, that after she completes it, she will not follow through with further study of the subject.

Many parents insist that their children follow in their footsteps. A carpenter may insist that his son be proficient in carpentry. The son may be able to learn all about it, but it may not be his strength – he may not be physically minded. Children in these circumstances sometimes develop strong feelings of inadequacy as they sense the expectations of their parents, but simply do not share with them the same inborn strengths. Parents often don't understand that their children might be totally different from them.

Work History

A review of past jobs, key events in your life, satisfying experiences, skills learned, friends made, and even unhappy times, helps you determine future directions. If your jobs have been dissatisfying, you don't want to repeat the pattern by accepting another one likely to lead in the same direction. A review of the past helps you to expand your self-knowledge, which in turn will help you determine the direction your life is taking and which direction you want it to take.

Where is the best place to start? If you are older, it might seem like a tall order to review your entire work history. Start with your most recent job. Write down each organization you worked for, and the various positions you held, along with the dates that correspond to them. Under each, identify your key responsibilities and major accomplishments. List the things you liked, and disliked about each position.

Accomplishments

Recalling your accomplishments and their significance will help you plan for the future.

What is an accomplishment? This is a completed job or project. It could be something that was completed in a day, or it might have taken years to complete. Selling a car is an accomplishment. It would be a more significant accomplishment if it were sold at a substantial profit. It would be regarded even more highly if the salesperson reported selling more cars in a month than any other salesperson in the dealership. Winning the salesperson award of the year is even more important as an accomplishment. Accomplishments take many forms – influential speeches; finding oil; organizing a workforce; building a house; reducing costs in a major enterprise; being a Girl Guide leader, or starting a new business. Accomplishments are usually time-limited, make a contribution, and use your abilities, experience and skills.

Academics

Our academic background has also been influential in our career direction to date, and may have significance for future choices. Without training in certain areas, you can't function in them. But training and academic achievement can be merely a confidence-giving springboard showing us that we do have the motivation to sustain an effort to its conclusion. Employers will often consider one's academic background as a basic building block for the career. This is especially true for people starting out in a career within a major organization.

Why did you choose the academic direction you did? Do you still use that knowledge in your work today? Do you need a particular academic background to get the job you want? Do you need to consider further education? What did you love (or hate) about being a student?

And suppose you didn't complete enough schooling? What are the implications for your career? It may limit you, but not as much as you think. Many highly successful people did not complete university degrees, and in some cases, they didn't even finish high school. (Success here is defined as achieving employment or financial goals, or personal success).

We do need to, somehow, constantly hone our skills and abilities. Some achieve it through a series of short courses. Others study on their own. Still others find their way in trial-and-error fashion, learning from their successes and mistakes.

Building Block 2. Your Future – Aspirations and Ideals

A major influence on our career direction comes from inside us, from our dreams, fantasies and idealism about what we would like to do.

As children we dream about what we would like to be. We may exaggerate in our daydreams but our fantasies will tell us a lot about what is most important to us, and give us clues to our future aspirations.

For example, some people fantasize about being strong and powerful, overcoming all obstacles by dint of their own brilliance or physical strength. Jobs as **managers and leaders** of others may be in their future.

Another person may think about being in beautiful surrounding dressed in the finest clothing, dining with, or talking to, elegant people. What does this suggest in the way of future interests? Perhaps this person will become a **clothing designer or architect**.

What about the person who dreams about being helpful to others or rescuing others when they are in trouble? Perhaps they will end up in occupations where they need to understand others and their motivations. They may make good **social workers, corrections officers, or psychiatrists**.

Fantasies about having unlimited resources lead many people to choose **high income** careers.

We should not discount the dreams we have had, or currently have. They can often be the fuel to ignite our energy to move in directions that are right for us. Looking at what we have done in the past, and whether we have enjoyed it or not, and linking these thoughts with the ideal occupations of our dreams, may lead us in new and interesting occupational directions.

When you identify your skills and aptitudes, you should, at the same time, ask yourself if you enjoy using those skills. Many people have a particular skill, but get very tired using it, and dream of the day when they leave it behind. Some who have professional occupations yearn for the day when they can move on. Some successfully develop jobs that build on their past experiences, but take them into brand new careers.

One imperative for an enjoyable career for most people is learning, adding to, growing and increasing the complexity of the work they do. Fulfillment comes from stretching their abilities, learning new ways of doing things, adding to their skill and from the challenge of totally new directions.

Many organizational leaders are well aware of the need employees have to take on more responsibility, or have more depth to their jobs, and so they help people to achieve this end. It is mutually beneficial for organizations to help people grow and develop, as it keeps their workforce motivated, interested and energized to be constantly productive.

Interests

You may already have had a series of jobs in your career. As people change jobs, they usually opt for work that is the same as, or similar to, what they were doing before. A few, however, change careers and make major shifts in the use of their talents.

You should test your interests against your skills and abilities. For example, an engineer may be enthralled with the idea of becoming a real estate salesperson, but might not take into account the major emphasis on selling in this profession. Or, a marketing vice-president might be interested in starting up a small business but might not understand either the loss of income involved or the amount of hands-on, detailed work it takes to get a small business started.

How can you ensure that you have taken *all* your interests

into account?

There are many systematic ways of determining your interests. A good interest inventory such as the **Strong Interest Inventory** mentioned previously or the **Career Occupational Preference System**[3] can help. Simply identifying your interests by paying attention to what enthuses you or how you tend to use your personal time is another way.

There is an excellent resource available at the public library called the **National Occupation Classification**[4]. It lists and describes all the jobs that people do. It also sets out, in general terms, the educational and skill requirement of each of them.

You need to be realistic yet forward-thinking about your goals, purpose, or mission for the next chapter of your life.

Building Block 3. Who You Are – The Person

Motivation

Some people are motivated for life to follow through on work that interests them or to be ever more expert in a unique area of science or technology. Other people are driven for shorter periods of time to give their total energies to a job or project lasting only a few months or years. Still others have a moderate amount of energy to put towards their work, and many times that's all that's required.

Being released from a job can shatter motivation levels leaving the

---

[3] Career Occupational Preference System, EdITS, 1982 has several versions of their instrument depending on the individual's needs or stage in his/her career.

[4] National Occupation Classification System is the Government of Canada's classification system of every occupation, including the qualifications one needs to enter, the usual skill and experience required as well as a generic description of the position. It brings together jobs that are titled differently but contain essentially the same content. The USA Federal Government has similar publications classifying occupations.

person affected to wonder why she gave so much to her job. She starts to ask herself questions. Why do I work? What do I want to accomplish? How hard do I want to work in the future? She knows the basic answers:

To provide for my family.
To earn as much money as I possibly can.
To travel and see new places in the course of my job.
To learn.
To be well recognized for my work.
Because everyone should work and be productive.
Because I love to (write, build, create, keep busy, help others).

These statements may be enough for some people as reasons to work. For others, though, there is something more to life, and they struggle to try and find this meaning. After being released, and looking back over their work history, some people get depressed wondering what was accomplished and whether they will be remembered.

As a person attempting to understand your own motivation, you are aware that many factors influence it. External factors such as how you are treated by others will definitely influence you. But, you can be as readily driven by factors in your own mind.

Reflecting on what drives you, what interests you, what depresses and de-energizes you, will help in understanding your own level of motivation, and what you need to do if you find that you have lost some of the energy you need to be effective in a new situation.

Values

This area requires us to be introspective about the importance we attach to intangible attitudes. We are more than our work history, our skills, or our aspirations.

Our values, beliefs, motivations and purposeful actions have a powerful influence on our decision-making and can't be put aside when it comes to determining our career direction.

Consider what is important to you. There are things we know we will do — things we might find challenging or exciting – and things that we would never do because they do not appeal to us or because they violate our deeply held beliefs about right and wrong. Knowing what you **can** do is important. But what are you **willing** to do? The answer to this depends on your unique style of living and working. To understand yourself, you should consider your personal or work-related values and preferences.

Each of us continually evaluates and makes judgements about the world around us. From childhood, we develop pre-dispositions that color our behaviour towards others. Our differing characteristics and personality traits lead us to think and behave along certain lines. As adults, we add to this mix the many positive and negative experiences we have accumulated over time.

Here are **12 work-related values** that influence the job a person will take and whether or not he/she will stay with it. Think about these for yourself – which two or three are most important of all to you? These have been taken from a much longer list. So, there could be other personal values that you hold as being very important that aren't on this list.

Achievement – doing things well; making an important contribution; seeing results; feeling satisfied about what I have done.

Advancement – moving ahead or "up" based on competence and hard work.

Affiliation – being in regular contact with others; attending social functions; having a sense of belonging; having many friends; working in groups and teams.

Balance - work, home and other pursuits take on equal importance; work is compromised at times to accommodate activity in other areas.

Competition – pitting my skill and experience against the skill and experience of others where there is a clear outcome identified in terms of winning or losing.

Creativity – developing new ideas, programs, plans and methods that have not been tried before; using creativity in writing, images or personal expression.

Helping Society – assisting a "cause"; making a lasting social contribution.

High Earnings – being viewed as "well-off" in comparison to others; acquiring what I want to have; having many options and choices resulting from high income.

Making Decisions – having the power to make policies and choices; being able to take action.

Personal Growth – taking work-related courses; having tasks that require me to learn; taking academic courses; pursuing knowledge; pursuing personal feedback.

Security – keeping my job; having good company benefits; knowing what the future holds; predictability in personal and managerial responsibilities.

Status – having a respected job title and position; associating with the elite.

Can you clearly identify two or three of these values as being very important to you? If you can, they will have a bearing on your choice of career, or next career. For example, if "Making Decisions" is highly valued, then you want to be on the look out for jobs where you can take independent action. Heading the remote branch office of a major corporation would be a good fit, or heading an IT function in a company where others rely totally on your decisions, because they don't really understand the technical aspects of what you are doing. Another possibility would be setting up your own enterprise.

Building Block 4. Who You Are – The Stresses and Strains

Stress[5]

We must take into account our ability to tolerate stress in making a career choice. Many jobs today place undue pressure on us to achieve, to get multiple tasks completed and to work effectively with everyone we encounter. Each of us needs to know our stress limits.

We tend to associate personal stress, anxiety and fear with weakness and failure. Because of this, these matters are often avoided in the context of career planning. But they should not be.

Fear

Some people suffer from immobilizing anxiety when they have to make certain kinds of personal contact, or when they get up in front of a group. Most of our anxiety, fear and stress relate to how we deal with others in interpersonal situations such as these. This can manifest itself in physical and behavioural ways: stomach cramps; an increased heart rate; perspiration; fidgeting; flushed face; cold hands; nervous behaviour; avoidance, and so on.

Typical fears and anxieties that lead to stress in people's lives include the following:

Fear of using the telephone
Fear of not being well enough prepared
Fear of things getting out of control
Fear of speaking in front of, or participating in groups
Fear of things going wrong
Fear of initial meetings with people

---

[5] The Psychology of Call Reluctance: Dudley, George W., Shannon L. Goodson, Behavioural Sciences Research Press, 1980 and Earning What Your Worth, 1995, by the same authors and Dr. David K. Barnett give excellent descriptions of some of the fear and anxiety people face in high stakes personal contact situations. They have categorized them and offer a series of solutions that can be self-applied to overcome these difficulties. Many of the fear types described here are taken from their material.

Fear about what others think
Fear that we might be ill prepared for some possible questions
Fear that we might not know how to explain our situation
Fear that we might come on too strong. This fear comes from the idea that we must always defer to the interests of others
Fear that we will be intimidated by contacts with people we consider our superiors because of their wealth, position, or power

People experiencing fearful feelings often think that their fears are justified by what they believe will actually happen to them. Essentially, they think that their fears are backed by FACT. The biggest insight a fear-ridden person can have is the realization that these fears reside internally and have no reality outside of him or her. It is how we think about our world, or what we believe to be the situation outside ourselves, that causes us to have fear.

As we plan for the next step in our career we need to take stock of this issue and how it impacts our lives. No one enjoys living in a constant state of dread about imagined consequences. As we proceed to the future, if our fears continue as a major concern, we need to take action to deal with them. There are many people who can help us address these issues and much has been written on the topic.

Strategies have been developed to help people deal with the stresses in their lives. Some strategies involve learning to relax; others use thinking approaches to cause us to look at things differently. One line of approach uses a "conditioning" approach to help people "eliminate" the stresses in their lives.[6]

---

[6] Ibid.

Health

Being healthy is also a key factor in our career success. Constraints on health can lead to limiting our vocational choices. We definitely need to consider the state of our health, as we consider all the other areas in our career choices.

There has been too much written on this topic to dwell on it here. We all need to consider the controllable parts of our own health and take advantage of our current knowledge to be as healthy as possible. If you don't have to consider your health as you career plan (because you are healthy) you should consider yourself blessed, and remind yourself that being in good health is tenuous at best for short periods of life, but can be extended by active participation in a healthy lifestyle.

Response to Change

The choice to change is taken from us by the employer who no longer needs us. Occupations dry up. Whole industries decline. It is more important than ever to know who you are, what you can do, and in particular, what skills and experience you have which are transferable to other settings. If the time arrives when you are released from employment you will be better off if you have considered some options in advance.

A healthy response to change is to constantly update yourself through reading, taking courses, studying, improving your ability with technology, and attending conferences in your field. One of the biggest difficulties for people who have not prepared for change is to find themselves out of a job, and also years behind their peers in knowledge and skill in their profession or trade.

One of the problems with constant change in our occupational environment is the difficulty of always having to deal with what we have left behind. It's not easy to forget or minimize former work settings, friends, communities, familiar types of work and even a familiar set of values as we attempt to move on to new challenges. There are always things about the past that we would like to retain in the future.

Building Block 5. Today's Work Reality

What immediate employment opportunities are "out there" anyway? Perhaps you hope to find a new job that is quite different from what you have been doing until now. Or perhaps you would like more continuity. The "work reality" is that many people choose to compromise in the course of a job search, based in part on opportunity availability. A number of factors can affect this.

Your attitude towards the workplace is important. If you believe a road is impassable, then it may be so for you. Another person, believing differently, might find a way through.

You may want to change jobs today. The reality is that it could take you many months to obtain new employment. Learning to search constructively for a new position will certainly speed up the process but there may be other factors preventing you from becoming employed quickly.

Below are four realities that job searchers face.

1.   **There is a scarcity of jobs in your area of competence.**

If the demand for people in your line of work is currently in decline you have two major options.

* Even in a declining field of employment there are still needs for people. Certain essential positions will be filled even while others are being eliminated. Jobs come available due to

promotion, retirement, death and people moving to other companies. You can actively seek employment in your field on the basis that, while there may be a slowdown, some positions are still available.

- You can transfer many of your technical and managerial skills to other areas. If you can manage people successfully in one environment, you can be a successful manager in another, quite different environment. Your technical skills as an engineer, accountant, information systems specialist, or in any other knowledge area will apply across a broad range of occupations. Choose to seek employment in another industry, not currently in decline, where you can use your skills.

2.   **There have been criticisms of your personal style, behaviour, and performance that may have a negative impact on your reputation in the workplace**.

Have a look at your previous performance reviews. If you don't have them, try to get copies from your employer or previous employer. If no performance reviews have been done, seek behavioural feedback from previous managers and co-workers. Are there any consistent themes about areas where you can improve, or about areas of your strengths? In either case, take this feedback into account as you formulate your plans.

The workplace is large. Most people will know nothing of your "failings" unless you tell them. Also, some of your shortcomings may be specific to certain situations, and could be considered strengths in another setting.

Each of us has weak areas and shortcomings as well as strengths. As you approach the future, put emphasis on your skills, experience and special aptitudes, and regard your shortcomings as challenges to be overcome.

3.   **You are not up-to-date in knowledge or technical skills now considered the norm in your industry**.

Particularly in technical areas (computer use, engineering, drafting, etc.), people often find they are no longer in touch. This may also apply to management or planning techniques. You can act to alleviate this situation.

You can, at least partially, fill the gaps in your knowledge through discussions with people considered to be in the vanguard in your field.

Review technical journals and recent industry research.

Take one or more short courses of the sort regularly offered by a variety of private and public institutions.

You might have to return to college or university to systematically update your knowledge and skill.

4.   **You are likely to experience some problems because of your age, gender, ethnic background or disabilities.**

While undoubtedly a factual basis exists for concern in these areas, the problems are often overstated. Sometimes, one of these four is used as the excuse for a less than adequate effort to change one's career.

Age – Today's job market increasingly needs older people. Small companies like to hire older people who require little or no training. Large companies hire them as consultants and mentors. Experience shows that older people who continue in the job market invariably find appropriate new employment when they carry out a comprehensive and energetic job search.

Young people often feel discriminated against because they lack experience or because of fewer jobs in a declining job market. Many younger job searchers start in positions which are not a good fit for their training but which give them working experience where they can demonstrate responsibility, communication and problem-solving skills.

Gender – There does appear to be discrimination against women for certain categories of employment.   Times are changing, however, with equal opportunity for all; more positions in every field of endeavour, and at every level, have women in their ranks.

Ethnic Background – Differences of language, culture, and religion may all play a role in causing a person to feel that others are discriminating against him or her.   Aboriginal people sometimes experience this kind of discrimination. People new to the country say they experience difficulties. In many cases, they need to make every effort to learn the language or improve their grasp of it. This is especially important, since communication is one of the key success factors in most occupations.

Discrimination is declining, however, largely by virtue of the number of people who fall into these categories. Every area of employment finds that it has well-qualified people holding positions of responsibility without regard for visible or less visible differences.

Disabilities – There are a great many people in the population with disabilities, when you include people limited by illnesses and hearing or sight loss, as well as people who are limited in the use of arms or legs. Some employment may not be available to those with certain disabilities. This is true if they lack the mobility, communication skills, or ability to work for long periods of time essential to the job.

Many people with disabilities work in 9 to 5 jobs. Some have difficulty with mobility. They benefit from the increased number of jobs that do not require employees to report to a specific work location. Still, many people want to have jobs that will allow them to go to a normal work environment where they can get to know their colleagues in a more traditional way.

At any rate, remember: discrimination solely on the basis of age, gender, ethnic background or disability is regarded as inappropriate, and in many North American and European jurisdictions, is illegal.

Building Block 6. Tomorrow's Work Reality

The career of our future may be very different from the one we hold today. While difficult to plan for, each of us needs to think about the implications of this changing future and have some contingency plans in place.

The rapid pace of change is reflected by the turmoil in most organizations. Companies restructure, reorganize, downsize, merge and disappear. Today, this turmoil seems more normal than the relatively short periods of corporate stability! In the process, companies must often release staff. This comes about, for example, when they have too many employees at a certain level or of a certain profession, or when they need to divest themselves of whole business units, or when they have to upgrade from outdated technologies or get out of certain fields of expertise.

If you hope to start or continue in corporate life, you may need enhanced personal coping skills to deal with so much change. How ready are you to face a continually changing situation? What is your attitude towards change in an organizational setting? What do you value?

It is in our nature to want stability, predictability and a dependable workplace. Many people starting out in today's world of work would hope to have a stable work environment for many years where they can have a benefits plan and regular salary increases. The reality is that instability, unpredictability and change are the order of the day. Young people know this is the case and have resigned themselves to coping in a world of wild swings of change. It's older people who find it difficult to cope with all this uncertainty.

Longer term, no one can predict with accuracy what the future will be like. However, people live longer. We know in Canada and the U.S. that a major demographic shift will result in many more retirees ten years from now being supported by far fewer people of working age. We also know that in the future people will work to an older age because of inadequate pensions and retirement savings, and because of the need for them in the workforce due to the above-mentioned demographic shift.

We know there are fewer people working as telephone operators, bank employees and farm employees. What will the 21st century hold for us for employment? Will there be more people working in health care, care for the aged, and in security work? Will the Internet spawn great increases in workers who create web businesses? Will global information transparency result in global businesses for small groups of employees? There are many possibilities.

Constructive Ways of Thinking about the Changing World of Work

- "**I will concentrate on knowing myself** – my skills and aptitudes – because no one can take my abilities from me."

- "**I know change is inevitable**, and that change may have a significant impact on me and even cause me to lose jobs several times in my career. This is not my fault. I just need to get on with my life in a positive way."

- **"I can keep control over my environment** by maintaining an objective attitude towards my present employer, my former employers, and my future prospects. When change affects me personally, it will not be because the world is *out to get me.*"

- "Since the world of work is clearly changing very rapidly, **I may not be totally up-to-date on the new ways of doing my job**, or even on some of the new types of jobs or areas of employment where I could fit. I should take whatever opportunities I can to look into and get training or education for other areas of employment or entrepreneurship."

CAREER GOAL

Some people seem to think it unnecessary to systematically set out a career goal. They feel they know where they are going and what they want. However, it is evident that more people formalize their aspirations. What are the advantages of doing so?

- It encourages you to be realistic about what you can achieve.

- It settles the issue for the time being.

- It gives you a target against which you can measure specific opportunities as they come your way.

- It can give you a long-term sense of direction.

- It gives you clarity of purpose as you talk to people in your network or as you meet with prospective employers.

- It helps you set parameters for testing your ambitions against the realities of the changing world of work.

- It can give you a sense of identity as a certain type of professional or worker in a specific field of endeavour.

Consider your goals for the future. Remember that nothing is fixed or permanent. You will go through many changes in the future. A specific goal for your immediate career will reduce your stress level and give you a more positive outlook as you face the changes the future will bring.

"MY FINAL PLAN"

Write out your career goal and plan based on the thinking you have done to this point. Items to put in the write-up:

A generic title of the position or opportunity. You may have more than one title, but try to limit your choices to no more than three.

A brief description of the tasks or responsibilities of the job or jobs.

Describe the work setting. In this description, include reference to:

- Your skills

- Your interests

- Your values

- Academic requirements

- Requirements for training

- Previous experience

Describe the availability of this kind of work and the competition you will face.

Practical matters:

- Physical location of the work setting

- Current and potential earnings

- Managerial style you prefer

Other factors you feel are important to achieving your desired position, or blocks to it.

If you have followed this through in a systematic fashion, you will now have considerable knowledge about yourself and about what careers or vocations make sense for you. A final step might be to simply write yourself a one- or two-page summary of what you have discovered about yourself, and what you intend to pursue from an occupational perspective.

CONCLUSION

Carefully thinking through your career plans is a good use of your time. Using a structured process will help to ensure that you don't leave out important considerations. Once you have your plan in place, check it out with people who know you well. They can tell you if it is realistic. There are always things other people know about us that we don't know about ourselves, and getting some feedback will help fine-tune the plan to make it one that has not only been thoroughly thought through, but is also achievable.

QUESTIONS AND ANSWERS

• *How do you evaluate your transferable skills?*

There are several options here. First of all you can carry out a self-evaluation. There are questionnaires available from career management firms that help a person consider all skill areas. Second, you can complete psychological career tests to help you more systematically assess your skill areas. Third, you can ask others who have worked closely with you to assess your skills. This can be done systematically by asking them to complete a 360-degree instrument, or it can be done informally through discussion with close associates. (Generally, 360-degree questionnaires are completed by people who know you well. A series of questions in behavioral, business, and skill areas are checked off on a scale of high to low. You complete the same questionnaire. The answers are compared to see how realistic you are about your competence as compared to how others see you).

• *Should you define yourself in the marketplace, or have the marketplace define you?*

You need to define what it is you want to do. Assessment of your skills, abilities, interests and strengths, will lead you to know the most appropriate direction for your career. You should take charge.

In fact, however, the marketplace will define you to some degree. People you get to know will have an impression of what you can do, and may invite you to join them. You may develop a reputation for being good in using a certain technology or as a manager in a particular area. It's hard to turn away from opportunities that are presented to you. But, if you have lost interest in these professions and jobs that others think you should do, you should stand your ground and hold out (if you can afford to) for the newer, more interesting and challenging work you would like to do.

- *If I don't want to always be changing my career, am I out of step with the way the world is going?*

Not necessarily. Some people continue in a single career throughout their lives. Perhaps they are fortunate that there is always something new to learn and new responsibilities to assume that add complexity to their daily tasks. People working in academic careers or research careers often follow a single line of endeavour, ever deepening it, throughout their work lives.

Ultimately it is up to you. Is the work you are doing routine, uninteresting and mundane? Even under these circumstances, some people would prefer to stay put, and get their excitement outside of work in their hobbies and personal pursuits. Unfortunately, as we have noted elsewhere in this book, even the person who does not want to change his or her career ought to be prepared for the time when the organization invites them to leave. Sometimes these are the people who are hardest hit by this big personal change.

3

EMOTIONS, CHOICES AND YOU

Mary, a public health nurse with the provincial government, knew her position was vulnerable. The government was making cutbacks, and she remembered some key words in the government position paper. "We are looking for efficiencies in child care services, in programs for the elderly, and in the ongoing work with unwed mothers," the paper said. Mary's work had been in eldercare. She had heard her own Director say on more than one occasion, "they're going to get rid of us, and farm this work out to private organizations."

The day she got the news of her termination, Mary was surprisingly calm. A counsellor had been brought in to meet her and explain the career advisory services available to her. She met with him for about 15 minutes and agreed to come into his office the next morning, even though she also had some momentary thoughts that maybe she would just take a few weeks off.

She remained calm and rational about her termination that evening at dinner. She joked with her husband about it. She made fun of the government for its lack of knowledge of what she really did. She said to her husband, a bit cynically, "well there goes 10 years of my life!"

And then it hit her. This job had been really important to her. Why had they released her and kept Alison, her office mate? She had 3 years more seniority than Alison. What would she do? Where could she get a job like the one she had, which she not only enjoyed but was good at. Who would hire her? What about money? She thought, "this is terribly embarrassing … how can I tell my mother and aunt Isabel, and what will I say to the people at our Monday night curling group?"

Suddenly she broke into tears as the full reality of the termination finally hit her. Up to this point she had been in denial, not really admitting to herself the enormity of this blow to her life.

The next morning at her meeting with the counselor, she was quite a different person from the calm, cool and collected person he had seen the afternoon before. His role now was to help her deal with her intense grief.

THE EMOTIONAL UPS AND DOWNS

In the course of a career search, most people experience mood swings ranging from discouragement to optimism and from depression to elation. This is normal and must be recognized and understood.

Losing your job triggers a wide range of emotional responses. You can expect to experience many of these same emotions even when you have initiated the change in your work status. While these responses differ for each person, they indicate that the normal process of **grieving** has begun. Those who deny the emotions associated with this process will often manifest signs of chronic unresolved grief for months or even years after the event. It is far better to permit yourself to mourn your loss in a normal fashion while the hurt is still acute.

The grieving process has several essential elements that normally occur, whether or not they are acknowledged.

• For many, the first reaction is one of **shock and denial**. The function of this reaction is to buffer the effect of the discouraging news. You might be saying, "I can't believe this is happening to me," or, "This won't really affect me that much." It is a normal reaction to a sudden piece of disturbing information. Minimizing its effect helps in the initial stages so that you can gradually begin to cope with the enormity of the loss or change.

• **Anger** is also normal as we try to **place blame** for what has happened. Anger fuels our aggression and even our creativity. From a positive perspective, this can help us to get things done on our own behalf. An angry person wants to find that person who is at fault. If someone is to blame, then they should be held accountable, or brought to justice. Sometimes people want to write angry letters finding fault and looking for a redress of their wrongs. Writing a letter can be quite useful to get the anger out of your system, but usually it is better if it is never mailed.

• Another stage is **bargaining.** Here the grieving person is essentially trying to cut his or her losses. Through bargaining, we minimize the hurt by trying to stop any more change from taking place. For example, at this stage you might make a bargain with yourself: "I may have lost my job, but I'm going to keep everything else – my other activities and relationships with family and friends – exactly the same."

- Some people become very isolated at a time of major change and sink into a state of **depression**. This is also a normal reaction. It flows from the full realization of the loss. If it is a job which is gone, you begin to realize that your loss includes not only the job, but also friends, projects, the former working environment, and the activities associated with it.

- Eventually, most people come to terms with the situation and **accept** it. This does not usually lead to enthusiasm, but rather to a sober recognition of the way things are.

During the Job Search

Most people experience many ups and downs in the course of a job search, precisely because of the cycle of grief outlined above. First, their job disappears whether through termination or choice.

Then, in the course of making many contacts to find another job, they discover that people have very little that is concrete to offer. Viable leads surface only once in a while. Most of these leads prove to be dead ends. This discouraging realization can re-ignite the flames of grieving.

Sometimes, you find you are a candidate for a job. You might, in your mind and emotions, put yourself in this new position before the job is actually offered to you. Then, if you don't get the job, you may have to grieve again the loss of employment, even though you never had it in the first place. For example you might blame yourself ("What did I do wrong?") or others ("They made a big mistake.")

Then, after you have finally found work, you may be surprised to discover that you feel quite strongly the loss of the things associated with being on the search for a job. If you were unemployed for a time, you may miss the freedom and ability to take initiative, the making of new contacts and daily networking activity. They were a heavy burden while the search was going on, but are missed now that the search has ended.

Being in Touch With Your Emotions

Perhaps you think these emotions are irrelevant. They are not. Indeed, to try to deny them makes you a candidate for job search burnout. You can reduce your stress by understanding ahead of time the steps in the cycle of grief. These emotions are normal and, by being aware of them, you can understand what you are going through. It is useful to go over your experiences in your mind. Talking to others about them can also help ease your hurt and frustration. The awareness this generates will help to gradually diminish the hurt and lessen its impact.

You might end up falling into an unhealthy state of chronic denial or anger if you try to act as though you are unaffected emotionally. At any rate, you will only be fooling yourself – everyone close to you will be aware that you are having a bad time even while you are trying to tell them, and yourself, that nothing is wrong.

Work with your grief. Allow it to happen. Seek to understand this process and accept it as normal. All of us are in a constant state of grief over the major and minor losses in our lives. We need to work with the emotions generated by our losses. They are an essential part of the growing and developing we must all continually do.

MAKING CHOICES

From very early childhood, choices and options of all sorts become available to us. We reject unpalatable ones immediately and narrow our range of choices. But we also let go of real possibilities, mostly because we lack the imagination or the motivation to follow through on them. An internal struggle takes place between the forces of the past, which say "follow the tried and true" and the siren voices of the future calling us to be more imaginative and to try new approaches.

After being released by a company, many people want to recreate their former job in a new setting. You might say, for example, "I am seeking a job similar to my last one – with about the same pay, the same responsibilities, using the same skills and experience." Thinking this way significantly narrows your options. Jobs are changing – the kind of job you had might be disappearing. If you were a middle manager, and positions like the one you held are being eliminated, then your chances of recreating that job might be very slim indeed.

Thoroughly review your options. Look at all short and longer term possibilities. Put consideration of future remuneration to one side for a time and consider what you like to do, and what you have dreamed of doing. Look at all the skills you have. Most people don't know all their options because they have not investigated the full range of different types of work available to them. You will have to do some research! As a good first step, talk to people who presently work in areas about which you know little, but which sound appealing to you. Investigating the ideas and work of others, combined with your own personal insight, can result in the identification of exciting new possibilities.

As for remuneration, you may be hoping to earn as much as, or more than you were before. But this may be unrealistic. People also have choices about how they use their financial resources and you can revise your thinking in this area as well. Many of us will take a substantial cut in pay to pursue a new opportunity that has other desirable features, such as enlightened management, a better work environment, future potential and work that is interesting or challenging, or both.

Sometimes we become trapped into thinking about our options in ways that reflect unproductive "mind-sets." We might be trapped in the mind-set of "status" and "prestige," and find it difficult to open our thinking to possibilities for which we are qualified but which would not accord us the social position we desire. An unwillingness to take any risks, or focusing only on compensation, exemplify unproductive mind-sets that can seriously limit our choices. Limiting beliefs like these can stop people from thinking seriously about going into business for themselves or even from vigorously promoting their talents to prospective employers.

FITTING YOUR JOB SEARCH TO YOUR PERSONALITY

Many job search manuals assume that it should be very simple for anyone to find new employment simply by following "*the formula.*" But even if there was one best way to search for a job, differences in personality will shape the actual job search procedures we use. For example, some advice-givers may urge you, as a first step, to get very well organized. But if you are generally not a well-organized person, you will not follow this advice. Another standard piece of advice suggests forcefully that you should make at least ten phone calls a day. Yet, for many people, making even one phone call a day is an enormous struggle. By nature, they find it very difficult to promote themselves over the phone.

Can you take advantage of your own personality, not follow the advice exactly, and still be successful in a job search? The answer is "yes, you can."

This does not mean that you can turn your job search into a pleasant and comfortable exercise. If you are searching hard for a new opportunity on a daily basis, you will experience discomfort and dissatisfaction from time to time. Also, there is no way to escape the inevitability of personal contacts with people. But perhaps you can tilt your approach in directions in which you have special talents.

Some introspection is required. You need to think about what you can do, what you find easy to do, and also what you might enjoy doing in connection with your job search. Some of the possibilities include:

- Phoning and discussing your objectives with people you know.

- Talking face-to-face about your objectives.

- Writing to prospective employers to broadcast your availability.

- Attending group workshops to share your concerns and get ideas.

- Reviewing the newspaper for suitable advertisements and responding to them.

- Talking to recruiters or placement agency personnel.

- Meeting people at social gatherings and briefly telling them your story.

- Making a group presentation in a setting where you can influence people and demonstrate your competence.

- Going to a coffee shop, restaurant or bar where you will meet people you know and can informally discuss your plans.

- Networking with people at a club, on the golf course, or at a fitness centre.

- Studying and continually renewing your knowledge in your area of competence. Some contacts will appreciate your expert knowledge.

- Researching business directories and other publications at the public library.

- Investigating new and different areas of work or

entrepreneurship.

- Teaching a course at a college, or conducting a training program.

- Surfing the Internet for contacts that might lead to new opportunities.

The one requirement of any job search is this: others must easily understand you and your objectives. This can be accomplished in a variety of ways. If you are a natural researcher and writer, you might want to consider using those talents to promote your objectives. Write to the appropriate person to convey state-of-the-art information. You want him or her to see that you are knowledgeable and well-qualified. Follow through with a phone call to see if the two of you can meet.

Job search necessarily takes you into the realm of self-promotion. You can't stay at home thinking about what you would like to do. Self-promotion includes contacting other people.

You must know what you have to offer so that you can easily write or speak about it to others. Most people achieve this self-knowledge in part by working through the process of developing a resumé. Chapter 2 on Planning Your Career will help increase your awareness of your skills, experience, values and potential career goals.

Assume that not even your best contacts know exactly what you can do. At the appropriate moment, you must be able to easily talk about your experience and accomplishments.

The ability to be friends with someone or to make a personal connection is important in a job search. You will not form deep, lasting friendships with many people – indeed, it may happen only once, and that might be with the person who hires you! But building a relationship is important in connection with each contact you make. There are various ways to do this, depending on your style of interacting.

- Use a person's name in the course of your conversation.

- Be curious about the other person – ask questions that show this interest.

- Smile while you talk. A smiling face causes others to feel included and appreciated.

- Do something for the other person. True relationships are reciprocal, requiring give and take.

- Respond honestly, even if this means disagreeing.

- Do your share of talking. Provide information that will be helpful to your contact.

- Don't over-talk. Your share, at most, is 50 percent of the "air time." Talking too much appears to the listeners as a lack of interest in them and what they have to offer.

Some people find that following the job searching "formula" fits them because they fit the formula. They are in the minority. The rest of us have to figure out what works *for us*. While looking for a new opportunity, you may have to do things that will make you feel uncomfortable. See this as positive – as helping you to build skills in new areas. You can come out of this experience a better, wiser person.

Don't beat yourself up if you can't make yourself follow "the recommended way." Instead, look at who you are and what you can easily do, then build out from this point.

QUESTIONS AND ANSWERS

- *How do you maintain a high energy level during the job search?*

We are energized by success, by opportunity and by doing the things we enjoy. If we feel under attack because of a job loss and become discouraged during a job search, we are very likely to become de-energized.

Monitor your energy level. Get exercise – it will help you increase your drive and vitality. Carry out activities where you are certain you will have success. Be involved in hobbies and other activities that take you away from job searching for enough time to re-energize and get a new perspective on your job search.

- *How do you deal with your emotions when asked why you were terminated?*

Prepare in advance for questions that might arise. Have someone ask you difficult and emotionally charged questions so that you can practice dealing with them. Keep your responses to any questions brief and to the point. Long answers often disclose your highly charged emotional state. Listen to your responses. Do you hear anger, blame, denial, self-deprecation or excuses in your response? If so you are giving away your emotional state. This would be all right if you were confiding to a counselor or close friend. But, if the person you are talking to can play a role in your re-employment, you don't want to be quite so emotionally candid.

Self-understanding is the key to responding effectively to questions that might cause you to be emotional. If you are aware of your emotional state, and how you may be affected by difficult questions, then you will be better at keeping the emotionality out of your responses, and respond factually, when it is important to do so.

4

THE JOB SEARCH SCHEDULE

Carl was always investigating and researching. After he lost his job in a downsizing, he didn't skip a beat. He immediately put his investigative skills into action and decided he would keep a detailed record of his job search. He also knew that keeping a close record would be motivating, as he would want to prove to himself that he could keep up a fast pace leading to re-employment.

He recorded every phone call, all visits and what they led to, ads he responded to and recruiters he contacted. He even charted where one lead took him to another and to a third and fourth. It did pay off.

He was re-employed in exactly the kind of job he wanted in just under three months from the day he actually started to search. Looking back, he saw that he had made 145 phone calls to potential contacts. Of these, 27 were people he already knew; the rest were leads he generated from those contacts or were "cold calls'" of names he obtained from directories or other sources. He replied to eight ads. Because Carl was somewhat specialized, it was difficult for him to find appropriate positions which were advertised. Nine recruiters met with him, after he had contacted 28. He identified 14 positions on Internet job sites, but 12 of these were in locations that he was not prepared to move to. He didn't write any letters on speculation, only ad response letters, and "thank you" letters or letters with a resumé that he sent at the request of people he contacted.

In the final analysis, three appropriate jobs were offered to him. He started discussions with two of them midway through his job search campaign. The third one became available in the final two weeks of his search. He took one of the earlier-offered jobs which came through a contact of a contact. He had talked to a business acquaintance from five years earlier who gave him two names. One of those people gave him a third name which was where the opportunity surfaced.

Carl felt his system had worked well, and that his records had played an important role in keeping him on track and motivated.

THE JOB SEARCH STRUCTURE

The first step is to establish a career goal (see Chapter 2). Then, transform this goal into a structure for carrying out a job search. Establishing a day-by-day plan of job search activities completes the third step.

Why is it so important to plan a job search schedule in detail? We can all, very easily, drift into bad habits during a job search. Many people find that searching for a job is not a pleasant task. It can be discouraging to continually call people, visit them, and ferret out possibilities – only to hear over and over that there is no job here and no chance there. The tendency is to procrastinate on making calls. You can end up waiting until the time is "just right" before starting or continuing the search – and perhaps never really get it started at all. Or you can start to get overly excited about the slightest prospect and, in the meantime, put other things on hold.

These are all delaying tactics. They give you reasons for not making the calls and visits which are so essential to an effective job search.

A schedule of job search activities will give you a structure against which to measure your day-by-day achievements.

A Plan for the Search

Map out a plan at the beginning of each week. Carry over activities from the previous week, including meetings you have scheduled and commitments you have made.

Establish the number of phone calls you plan to make during the week. Include the precise hours when these calls are to be made. The *quantity* of calls is extremely important. Calls to people you already know and calls to those you have not met are of equal importance. As time goes by, you will find that the number of calls to people you know will decline until finally almost all of them connect you with strangers.

The objective of a phone call is almost always the same. You want to set up a face-to-face meeting with the person being called. Much has been written on how to handle these calls. When handled well, you should be able to persuade three people to see you for every ten who speak with you on the phone.

Establish a schedule with time slots for personal meetings and make every effort to fill each slot. Aim at having a minimum of six meetings per week if you are searching full-time. If you are working, then you will have to fit your plan to when you can take breaks from your job.

You will need time to do research. This includes checking for advertised positions, reading the newspaper for information, combing the directories for names of people to contact and time spent looking for leads on Internet job boards and web sites. You should give this activity a lower priority, however, than actually talking to people by phone or in person. You can always schedule time in the evenings, or early mornings, or on weekends for this research. This will leave time during business hours to make those all-important personal phone calls.

At the end of each week, assess how well you have done. It sometimes helps to have someone to report to, such as a friend, a family member or, if you are out of work, a career consultant. Reporting regularly to another person can force you to be accountable and help you live up to the standards you have set.

We mentioned in Chapter 1 that a job search is a highly personal matter. Each of us approaches it differently. There is no "magic way" that everyone can follow. Nevertheless, the question keeps coming up: "What makes up a 'formula' for success?" While we know some people will not consider the following formula useful, others have succeeded by using it. It is of particular benefit to the person who is not working and has full-time to search for an opportunity.

Here is a winning formula, then, for the person who wants to limit the length of his/her job search:

Make 15 "dials" every day to people you have never contacted before. A dial is just that – an attempt to get through, leaving your phone number. This method presumes that you will normally be able to actually talk to only a portion of the people you dialed.

Expect that you will eventually speak with ten of the people dialed. This is an average number, and may vary considerably.

Expect that three of the ten will agree to see you for a short interview. You can carry out a phone interview with some of those who won't agree to meet you personally.

Expect to identify one possible job for every ten personal visits. Some of these opportunities will not be a good fit for you and, for some, you will be one of many applicants.

Expect to be offered one job (possibly after several interviews) for every six you identify.

In other words, expect to make roughly 300 calls to reach 200 people by phone, of which 60 will agree to see you. In these 60 visits, you will identify 6 opportunities, of which you are likely to be offered one that is appropriate for you.

A vigorous *process* of job searching invariably leads to job possibilities. A low level of activity results in fewer leads. This is a direct relationship. Those people who are serious about finding a new job quickly will put aside their fear of calling and push past the lowered self-esteem they might feel if they lost their last job, and **make those calls!**

PERSISTENCE IN A JOB SEARCH – WHEN TO PUSH OR BACK OFF

You might be asking, "Should I call now, or wait?" When the time has come to follow up on a contact, what should you say?

There are several target markets for your calls. Each may require a different answer to these questions.

Responding to Job Advertisements

After you respond to an ad, it is appropriate to call the firm or person who placed it. Make the call about two weeks after the ad appeared. The point of this call is to see if your response was received, if they need any additional information and if they have made plans to interview candidates. You should also reiterate your strong interest in being interviewed.

Make a second call regarding the position if the advice you were given during your first call does not appear to be happening. For example, the company recruiter might say that you will hear from him or her within a week. If you don't, then it is appropriate to wait a further week and call again. In this call, you can check whether a hiring decision has been made and find out whether you should still consider yourself a candidate. If so, request an interview.

Subsequent calls are only appropriate if the other person has encouraged you to make them.

The above sequence would normally end your initiative regarding ad responses. Additional calls might be interpreted as pushy, annoying or inappropriate. In the final analysis, an organization may hire anyone they wish, and they do not have to tell you anything about it.

Read more about Ad Responses in Job Search Methods, Chapter 6.

Networking

You need to make many contacts – that is, to be continually *networking.* The more people you connect with, the more opportunities can come your way.

There are many different ways in which networking can take place. Here are four.

With Friends

How frequently should you get in touch with the same friend during your job search? This can be handled in many different ways and will naturally depend on how well you know him or her. Three contacts are often sufficient. You make personal contact by phone, then follow up the call with a personal visit and a thank you letter. If your search stretches out, you may want to get back in touch with people you called early on, just to let them know you are still looking. You should not do this more than once every two months or so – with some friends, once every three or four month will be even better.

Remember that you aren't looking for sympathy or counseling. You don't want your friends to feel guilty about your job search. Your call is simply to give information. You might say something like: "I'm calling to let you know that I'm still on the job market. My search is taking a while, which is not uncommon. I have made some very good contacts but have nothing definite so far. If you hear of anything, or if you have any further suggestions for me by way of information or contacts, I would certainly appreciate it if you would let me know. I know you are unlikely to come up with something at this very moment. If you think of anything, though, please give me a call. It's easiest to reach me at . . ."

Cold Calls

After the initial call, should you call back to people you don't know? This depends on how the call went. If the call opened the door for you to visit this contact and the visit went well, then ask if you may keep in touch. In such a case, phone back three weeks later to thank him or her for the information you received, and to report on your search. A follow-up "thank-you" letter is also recommended. It can serve two purposes: to show true appreciation for the time taken, and as a reminder to this contact of you and your objectives.

Broadcast Letters

In today's job market, there is little point in sending out letters advertising your availability unless you follow up each one with a personal phone call. On the other hand, you can get as much as a 30 percent interview rate from an effective letter followed by a phone call. The telephone contact should come between ten days and two weeks after sending the letter. All letters should be addressed personally. Don't use the "Dear Sir/Madam" approach.

Begin the phone call by asking the recipient if he or she remembers getting your letter. Don't be flustered if your letter has not been read or even seen. Talk about your job search objective and ask if you might meet in person.

After an Interview

After you have had an interview for a real job, how would you handle further contacts with your prospective employer? At the end of the interview itself, ask the interviewer about the time line for the recruitment process. You can use this information as your guide for calling back. If you have not heard anything three days after the deadline indicated for getting back to you, you should call to see what has been happening and when, or whether, you can expect further word. You might ask if the organization needs any further information about you or whether it would be useful for you to meet other key players.

If you cannot seem to get a straight answer, it is probably wise to assume the worst. The organization may be negotiating with another candidate and may not want to tip their hand, or they may simply not want to disappoint you by telling you over the phone that you are no longer in the running.

The Law of Diminishing Returns

The most important call is the first one. Each subsequent call to the same person reduces your chance of identifying an opportunity. Avoid going on a "hope trip" by continually calling the same people, or by indulging the fantasy that your friends or existing contacts are somehow going to come through for you. Because of the "Law of Diminishing Returns," it is important to continually make new contacts in the course of your job search.

QUESTIONS AND ANSWERS

- *How do I deal with my tendency to procrastinate?*

Each person has to look at the enemy within and decide how he/she is going to wage war on it. Making commitments to other people can be useful, because now the accountability goes beyond yourself and if you don't follow through you may find yourself making weak excuses. Some people even go so far as to make a contract with another person to hold them accountable for what they say they are going to do.

For some people, it can also be useful to spell out a plan in writing for what they will achieve, week by week. If you look back, and discover that you have not maintained your commitment you need to evaluate why. There may be good reasons, but it may also be your explanation as to why you are not getting anywhere in your job search. Deeply examining all of your motivations and failings may simply lead to further reasons to procrastinate. For many people it is not useful to fall into this trap, but rather it is better to give themselves a solid internal tongue-lashing and get on with the plan!

- *How do you establish appropriate target lists of people or organizations?*

You don't have to be as discriminating in making up a target list as you may think. There are many stories of the elderly neighbor and the out-to-lunch relative who have been the key contacts, which led to other contacts, resulting in finding a real job. Your list can also include relatives and friends who know virtually nothing about what you do.

If you want to search in a more systematic and business-like fashion, you can easily identify contacts from the directories of various industries. Since these are invariably out-of-date, you will occasionally find that the person you are trying to contact has changed jobs. This simply provides an opportunity to talk to his or her successor, and to contact the original person at his or her new place of employment.

Establishing a list of contacts is simply an exercise in creativity. There is no end to possible contacts and sources.

- *What do you do when you exhaust your contact list?*

You can't possibly contact all the people who could be helpful to you. If you have positioned yourself to only talk to people currently in the industry you want to get into, and who are at a certain level, in a certain location, then maybe you can claim to have exhausted your contacts. But, it is a big mistake to constrain yourself in this fashion because, as explained in response to the question above, leads can come from the most unusual places.

- *How should you structure an Internet search?*

The Internet has an unlimited number of job boards and employment sites. Many companies are now listing any opportunities they have on their web site.

To effectively take advantage of the Internet you need to do some preliminary work to find out which job-listing sources are going to be of most use in your particular search. You will find that some have many jobs, but none in your geographic area, or in your particular specialty. If you know organizations you would like to work for, you can go to their sites to see if they have jobs listed, or if they provide a means to apply even if they currently have no jobs available.

All your efforts to use the Internet should happen at times when it is impossible for you to carry out contacting, which is the most important part of your job search. Don't spend hours during the day, or even days trying to carry out a search through the 'Net. The payoff is not there in comparison to the personal contacting you can do.

However, you may discover a job on the 'Net that looks interesting. What is to prevent you from personally calling people at that company to find out more about it, and ultimately getting an interview through personal contacts? Applying by resumé on the Internet will not be nearly as effective as meeting people, resulting in a request that you leave your resumé with commitments for follow-up.

5

Résumé Preparation

DOES YOUR RESUMÉ COMMUNICATE?

Despite all the books, articles and lectures with tips on resumé writing, few resumés communicate effectively. The reason lies in how we view the resumé. Most people see it merely as a vehicle for giving information they think might interest a potential employer. However, taking this approach misses the point.

An applicant for a position as a consultant for a major management consulting firm responded with a one-page letter. In the letter, which used about three-quarters of the page, she responded well to all the items that were in the newspaper advertisement. The experienced recruiter received this very favourably. It communicated effectively, even though it did not follow the standard formats, and no resumé was included. She got the interview.

Information can be offered without being communicated.

Communication happens only when the receiving person has begun to digest the information being offered. In other words, communication requires at least two people – the sender and the receiver, who completes the transaction and *turns the information into communication.* Because of this, it is vitally important that you place yourself in the shoes of the receiver. What your resumé communicates will depend to a large extent on the receiver's positive or negative reaction to it. Here are some things that might positively or negatively influence a receiver:

- *Length.* The recipient might not have the time or commitment to spend more than a few seconds on a particular resumé. A long one is often an immediate turn-off. A short, precise resumé might attract more attention.

- *Layout.* It is well known that when people read they tend to pick out certain words, phrases and emphasized points. If your resumé has many long paragraphs with little separation or emphasis, it may discourage the receiver.

- *The font.* In order to meet the criterion of having a short resumé, some people use small type fonts and leave little white space. This will turn off many readers who find it impossible to read without a magnifying glass. Use type fonts normally used in reports and letters. It is better to have it a little longer and readable than crammed together simply to meet the objective of being on two pages.

- *Content.* Readers are looking for certain types of information. They want to know about your work experience, educational background, key areas of accomplishment and community leadership. In some cases, it may serve you well to custom-make a resumé for a particular situation. Your resumé could work against you, possibly disqualify you, if you have not clearly described the experience and background (which you may have) needed by the recruiting organization.

- *Appeal.* Resumés that are photocopies of photocopies, or bear the marks of having been through several fax machines, will make an unfavourable impression on the reader. This may communicate a careless approach to the receiver. It may also deliver the message that the job searcher does not really care about any particular job and is mass-mailing the resumé. Those looking for applicants will find it easier to not consider this person.

- *Unique ideas.* Job searchers sometimes think they can cut through to an interview by being unique. They tell stories in their resumés; they add a picture; they bind it in an expensive or colourful folder. All these techniques, and ones like them, create communication problems. When the unique approach enters the mind of the receiver, it must face all of his or her values, biases and experiences – and even the mood of the day. Every now and then an employer will react positively: "Isn't this innovative – I think I'll interview this person." But the overwhelming response will be negative, and in almost every case a unique approach will work against you.

Give your resumé the "other person" test. Let other people review it and tell you how they react to it. Look for the emotional impact of your resumé as much as the impact of the information. You want the receiver to be thinking: "this resumé is easy to read and understand; if this person thinks as clearly and succinctly as she writes, then we might have a fit."

RESUMÉ PREPARATION

You are in a hurry to prepare your resumé. Perhaps you need it in the next day or two for an opportunity that could come your way. While it is important to get your resumé in place as soon as possible, it must also be done well. Most people go through many drafts to get to the final version.

There are several different types of resumés. Below is a quick guide to preparing a reverse order, chronological resumé.

Remember that prospective employers use the resumé more to screen out unsuitable people than to select qualified candidates. For this reason you should eliminate, as much as possible, any extra information, which could receive a negative review from the person reading it.

Your resumé should include the following elements:

Name, Address, Telephone (home, office, fax), e-mail. These should appear at the beginning. Prospective employers do not need to know your height, weight, age, social insurance number or the names of other members of your family.

- *A profile.* In a few words a profile encapsulates your experience. It usually starts with a generic title. For example, "An Accounting Manager with 10 years experience directly involved in all aspects of budgeting and financial reporting."

  Or as an alternative,

- *An Objective.* An objective states very briefly what you are targeting at, which might be somewhat different from your recent duties. Sometimes this statement is presented in a covering letter. It should not be more than a sentence or two in length. It very generally sets out the experience and skill you have which backs up the claim that you are qualified in this area. You should avoid making unverifiable claims such as, "a self-starter," "highly motivated," or that you have "excellent interpersonal skills." Such claims are usually not provable. Also, job searchers have overused them.

Here is an example of an objective statement: "Seeking a position as a Human Resources Manager building on 15 years of experience in various facets of the Human Resources function. Experience includes recruiting, salary administration, setting up a performance review system and organizing management training programs."

• *Your work experience.* Present this in *reverse chronological order* putting your most recent experience first. Provide more detail about your recent jobs than about your earlier jobs. Identify the year you started each job and the year it ended. You don't need to show the month of the year that you finished or started a job. Include accomplishments or responsibilities and quantify them as much as possible. It's not necessary to indicate to whom you reported. Go no more than 20 years into the past. Experience prior to this time can be covered in a generalized statement. "Prior to 1983 I held front-line positions as a ____ and a ____."

• *Accomplishments.* Sometimes it is valuable to set up your accomplishments in a separate grouping. They can be grouped under each position held, or in a functional resumé (see "Types of Resumés" later in this chapter), they may have their own separate section and may be set out according to the significance of each accomplishment, the most important coming first.

Here are examples of what we mean by quantifying an accomplishment.

- "Increased profits by 15% in two years by reducing costs in the accounting department."
- "Carried out 20 major promotional events which enhanced the image of our company. The company believes this helped in the 2% increase in market-share in the subsequent year."
- "Saved the company $100,000 annually by developing and implementing a new benefit plan for employees."

Quantification can take the form of increase in profits, decrease in expenses, speed of accomplishment, number of people involved, accuracy, reduction in errors, etc.

Not all accomplishments can be quantified, but they can still show results. Here are examples:

- "Input a manual filing system onto a computer database, drastically improving the accessibility of all files, including rarely used files."
- "As a member of a productivity task force, played a role in establishing new ways of communicating internally that resulted in improved morale."
- "Chaired a Quality Control Committee for the training department which set up standards for all educational and training programs in the company."

- *Special skills.* This section is especially relevant if you have the technical ability to operate certain equipment or to carry out highly specialized technical tasks such as reading technical material, programming computers, or working with software. This is where you would identify the various computer programs that you have used in the past.

- *Educational background.* This should include formal education, such as the degrees or diplomas you have earned as well as the short courses you have taken. It is not necessary to date the completion of courses. You should separate the programs that have taken years to complete from those that were taken in a few hours, days or weeks.

It can actually work against you to indicate the dates of completed degrees if they were completed a long time ago – the reader might wonder if you are really up-to-date in your field. If you have taken a vast array of short courses, include only those that are most relevant to the position you are seeking.

- *Significant affiliations, both past and present.* This can show the kind of leadership you have given to the community. You don't want to only show you are a joiner. Place emphasis on the official offices you have held and the special roles filled. Indicate here significant professional designations that you hold as an engineer, accountant, etc.

Significant Turn-offs

- "A senior executive with 25 years experience . . ." To a 35-year-old recruiter, anyone with that much experience is also very old, maybe too old for the job.

- "A high degree of interest in the field of . . ." This might leave the reader wondering whether you have any experience to match your apparent interest.

- "A perfectionist . . ." Then why have you allowed the typos and spelling or grammatical errors the reader has found in your resumé? Such errors rule people out of many a competition.

Dog-eared, messy looking resumés usually end up in the permanent, round files on recruiters' floors.

Common Problems

- Most people leave hobbies and other personal matters out of resumés. Sometimes one or more of these items will raise questions or eyebrows. "She has many hobbies; does she have time for work?" "I see he loves to hunt. Personally, I'm opposed to that hobby on ethical grounds."

- The ideal length for a resumé is two to three pages. A one-page resumé can also be well received. However, recruiters and employers tend to skim the long ones.

- Don't include a photograph or other visual illustration. You can never be sure what this will communicate to the receiver.

- Don't bind your resumé in a special cover or jacket. This will generally cause difficulty for anyone who is very quickly screening dozens or hundreds of resumés.

- Don't include salary expectations. If you wish to deal with remuneration in a covering letter, you can use a turn of phrase such as, "My salary requirements are flexible and well within the range generally paid for this type of position."

- Don't include references. In your covering letter, consider phrasing it something like, "I will be happy to provide references if my application is to be considered." The exception to this rule is the academic setting. In these institutions, recruiters usually expect that you will include references with your first letter of application.

The reason for not including references for business

organization applications is to preclude the company checking references before they talk to you. No matter how favourable your references may be, you don't know exactly how they will handle specific questions. Also, if you are still on the job, you may not want your existing organization to know you are on the lookout for a new position.

- Don't try to "sell" yourself through the written word. Set out your resumé as clearly and succinctly as possible. It can reinforce your personal interview or introduce you, but it alone will not get you a job.

TYPES OF RESUMÉS

Different types of resumés have different requirements. The following is a list of eight types and the sections they include. Note the different ordering of the sections in each type. Also identified here are special concerns with resumé scanning, and with e-mailed and faxed resumés.

Chronological Type

Name, address, phone numbers, e-mail

Descriptive initial statement of your objective(s) or profile

Work experience – most recent to least recent, including achievements

Educational background

Special technical skills

Other involvements (community associations, professional affiliations, political associations, etc.)

Publications (if appropriate)

Functional Type

Name, address, phone numbers, e-mail

Descriptive initial statement of your objective(s) or profile

Important achievements (listed according to categories. List first those you wish to reproduce or apply in a new job)

Special technical skills

Work experience – most recent to least recent

Educational background

Other involvements

Publications (if appropriate)

Targeted Type (a specific resume written for a specific purpose)

Name, address, phone numbers, e-mail

Descriptive initial statement of your job search objective relating to the target

Work experience or important achievements – this will vary from position to position depending on the relevance of your experience or achievements in each case

Educational background

Special technical skills

Other involvements

Publications (if appropriate)

Recruiter/Placement/Agency Type

Name, address, phone numbers, e-mail

Descriptive initial statement of your job search objective or profile

Educational background

Work experience – most recent to least recent, including achievements

Special technical skills

Other involvements

Publications (if appropriate)

Academic Type

Name, Address, Phone Numbers, E-mail

Name and Address of current institution where you are working (if this is the case)

Statement of your objective.

Educational background
> Degrees, theses titles, names of theses supervisors and their positions.
> Areas of specialization and competence.

Work experience in reverse chronological order.

Publications
> Published articles, books, book reviews, conference presentations, invited presentations, special lectures.

References
> This is the only type of resumé where it is recommended to include references in the resumé itself.

Scanner Type

A resumé that you suspect will be "scanned" can follow any of the above resumé formats. Take into account the reasons why organizations use scanners.

The programmed scanner searches for words and phrases the recruiter has keyed in to help find a few resumés to actually read. It is very important for the job searcher to ensure that key words and phrases about his or her experience appear, preferably in the first 2 pages. Read the advertisement and use phrases that are being used in the ad. For example, if you are an HR professional, and, if the word "personnel" is being used in the ad instead of "human resources" to describe this function, be sure to use this language. Use a variety of words and phrases to describe your skills, responsibilities and achievements so that the scanner will have more opportunities to match the words in your resumé with the words and phrases programmed in by the recruiter.

Other points about Resumé Scanning.
- Making your name very large on the resumé may make it unreadable by the scanner. Keep it under 18-point size.
- Other type should be no smaller than 9 and no larger than 12 point size.
- Put your name on each page.
- Don't underline – this may confuse the scanner. Don't use lines anywhere.
- If using "bullets" to identify points, ensure they are solid so as not to be mistaken for letters or numbers.
- Use high quality, white or light coloured paper.
- Use traditional fonts.
- Don't staple pages together – a paper clip is better.
- Avoid using fonts that touch each other.
- Use a laser printer – not a dot matrix.
- Don't use columns.

- Don't box statements.
- Don't abbreviate words. However, it is appropriate to use the usual letters for degrees.

E-mailed Type

The same formats for resumé preparation can be used, i.e., chronological, functional, etc. However, the text of the e-mailed resumé should contain only text – no graphics, no special fonts, no special margins or anything else. This will ensure that it will be received without errors, or without absent information. It will, however, look very plain, but people who want resumés sent to them by e-mail have come to expect them to be no-frills documents.

Prepare the document in a word processing program, and then paste it into the text of your E-mail, rather than sending it as an attachment. This gives additional assurance that it will actually arrive. Sometimes the computer you are sending it to can't open an attachment, or the person using the computer does not know how to open attachments and it just gets sent to the garbage bin.

If you are uncertain about how your resumé looks as it comes out the other end, carry out a test run. Send it to yourself or to the computer of a friend and see how it turned out.

There has been much written on this topic. If you need further information, visit the public library or seek the information you need from the Internet.

Faxed Type

When you fax a resumé you expect that it will be received exactly as you sent it. You can send any type, - chronological, functional, targeted or others through this medium. It's fast and convenient.

However, it does have drawbacks. The person doing the faxing does not have as much control as he or she would like. Your excellent faxed instrument may arrive with lines through it, or be fuzzy in some places, or even have pages missing because of transmission difficulties, or because of the quality of the receiving fax. It is always wise to back up your faxed resumé by mailing, or personally delivering one. You can indicate on your faxed copy that an original will follow by mail. In the cover letter with the mailed copy, ask the receiver to substitute this one for the one you faxed.

HOW TO USE YOUR RESUMÉ

You have now prepared your resumé. You feel positive about it. Perhaps you even feel that it is the key to your job search. Nevertheless, no matter how good it is, it will not get you a job.

You need to have a resumé. Indeed, you may need several, each emphasizing different aspects of your background. But the job itself will come as a result of personally presenting yourself to a prospective hiring authority. The development of your resumé is an excellent process for clarifying and fine-tuning the focus of your career, but in the final analysis, you might not use it as much as you expected.

When you reply to an advertisement, it may be necessary to send a letter and your resumé before you can actually see anyone. When this happens, it will be scrutinized very carefully to see whether you can be eliminated from the competition. After all, a shortlist of candidates is being developed – the company wants to interview only a small number of eligible individuals.

Resumés often provide some excuse for *not* considering people. You might not have the precise qualifications, for example, or you might be missing some needed experience. Having too much experience can also be a deficiency at times. Whoever reads it might also put it aside for not being prepared in the way he or she prefers. Sometimes it will be more advantageous to send a good letter outlining how you could do the job and the specific qualifications you have, instead of a resumé.

Do your best to arrange personal meetings with the people on your contact list. When that isn't possible, present yourself by telephone. Send or take your resumé to them after this initial contact. As a result of the discussion you may want to change it. For example, you may realize during your discussion that the job requires certain experience, which you have not recorded, even though you have it. You need to add this experience to your resumé before sending it to the contact.

If it hasn't been sent in advance, you will be asked for your resumé when you go to a job interview, and you should ensure that you have it with you. Delay giving it to the interviewer as long as possible, so that you can form a personal relationship without the barrier that a written document will often create. The interviewer might feel obliged to read and react rather than engage in a direct conversation with you.

Sometimes you can use your resumé to form a bond with your contacts. You can ask them to react to it. Do they like the format? The length? Do they have any comments or criticisms that might be helpful to you? This can be of service to you in improving it and will also give the people providing the feedback the feeling they have contributed to your job search.

QUESTIONS AND ANSWERS

- *How long should it take to prepare an excellent resumé?*

Usually people go through several stages of preparation, or in some cases, preparing several resumés for different purposes. Initially, there is the process of simply gathering information about yourself. Then, you need to select an order in which to put the information. Preparing the profile statement is another step. Editing and fine tuning, adding and deleting usually take some time. Generally, a person who works at its development consistently should have a resumé prepared in 10 hours, but the time might be spread out over one or two weeks.

A resumé, however, is never a finished product. Sometimes it is necessary to tweak it a bit to reply to a particular ad, or for the benefit of a recruiter. Improvements will be made as a result of the comments of friends and business associates, or from advice provided by those to whom you applied. Also, the job searcher may want to develop a very short resumé for some purposes, perhaps only one page in length. He may want to have a longer one, going into detail, for the person who wants this information because of serious consideration for a position.

- *How do you deal with gaps in employment history?*

Many people face this difficulty. At least four reasons come to mind.
- There have been lengthy periods of unemployment
- The person was at home taking care of a family
- An illness forced the person out of the workforce for a time
- The searcher has moved from job to job so frequently that he or she does not want to record all these changes

In some cases, the best approach is honesty in a simple statement appearing on the resumé. Identify the time period, and put "Raising a family and looking after a home." Another response: "A period of study and travel", or "a protracted illness from which I made a full recovery."

Sometimes people don't know how to explain their situation. Using a functional resumé may help because you can set out achievements and responsibilities held, and highlight them without identifying their dates within your work history. You can even essentially leave out your work history, or just have a few sentences about the actual firms you have worked for. This, however, is not popular with people who receive resumés. If it works to get you in the door, then you are in a much better position to talk about what you have been doing, and the reasons for gaps. You can say that you will provide a chronological resumé if this is desired, as long as the recipient now has an appreciation for the gaps.

- *What other documents are useful to have in a job search?*

Sometimes it is useful to have a one-page profile to hand out to people who are good contacts for you, but not necessarily potential employers. Prepare a business card. It is also useful to have standard cover letters and thank you letters.

If you are attempting to go into an entrepreneurial venture as a consultant, prepare a brochure which describes who you are, what you can do and the area of consulting you plan to undertake.

- *Should you apply for jobs where you are short on experience?*

The short answer is "yes." People are transferring across disciplines and job types all the time. Professionals become managers. People with single-function responsibilities take on other functions. On the resumé you must be able to highlight "transferable skills." Perhaps you have not actually been a manager in the past, but you can likely show where you have managed specific functions or activities and identify some accomplishments. The best kind of job is one where you are reaching out to do more, to have a more complex job than your present or last one. If you are totally competent for the job you have applied for, you may soon become bored with it. It isn't providing the opportunity to learn, or grow your talents and abilities.

• *Are there times when it is inappropriate to give out your resumé?*

You should never give it to someone at the start of a job search conversation. Do you want them to look at your document or get to know the real you? Hold on to your resumé as long as you can. Leave it behind, as you leave the interviewer or send it later. Of course, this may not always be possible, but delaying the presentation of your resumé will benefit you in your relationship building.

• *To restart your career at a lower level, should you de-skill your resumé?*

You may turn off potential employers by presenting a resumé that shows experience which is clearly beyond what they need. The reaction is, "how long will this over-qualified person stay?" If you are definite about wanting to come into a lower level position then leave out those items that will be received negatively. In the objective statement, make it clear that you are looking for the lower level position. State clearly your reasons for doing this. For example, you might say, "I am seeking an opportunity to have a growth experience by entering another business. This is more important to me than having a more senior role, at this point in my career."

Be truthful about the positions you held and their titles. But you can leave out accomplishments or key responsibilities that may cause a reaction that you are very much overqualified for the position. If there are qualifications, such as in the technical area, that you have, and that are required by the position, make sure these are emphasized.

Remember: *in the final analysis, people hire people – not resumés.*

6

JOB SEARCH METHODS

Jaya successfully got through to Frank Summers, the head of the IT Department at Ronars Corp. She had often dreamed about the possibility of working for Ronars. They were well established and known for their advanced systems in tracking, invoicing and customer database information. She was an expert in the customer area, and her present company had given her special recognition for innovations she had developed to ensure effective and ongoing contacts with existing customers and prospects.

Frank didn't know her, but he had a personal policy of seeing people who contacted him. He wanted to keep on top of who was available. His IT professionals were constantly being offered attractive jobs by other firms and he liked to know of qualified people he could recruit quickly.

Jaya was very nervous about visiting with Frank. Now that she had the meeting, what would she say? He said he had no openings at the present time. She knew what the objective was: to simply make a good impression and be known to Frank so that if he did have a need, he would think of her.

To interfere with her own work as little as possible, she had arranged to meet him at 4 p.m. Frank seemed ok with the time as well.

She racked her brain about how to handle the interview. She wanted to be brief, but find out about how the company and its IT Department functioned. She wanted to leave with a feeling that she and Frank had really connected.

She determined to ask him about the current objectives of Ronars, and how the corporate objectives impacted on the IT group. She also wanted to make sure he knew her skill base and how she could be useful to him, if there was an opening. She would emphasize the work she had done with the customer database.

At their meeting, Jaya realized that she was not prepared for Frank's questions. Why did she want to leave her company? (She didn't). Did she have expertise in local area networking? (Farthest from her interest or ability). Did she know some of his contacts in the industry? (She had only heard of them). She had a sinking feeling that this whole interview was going in the dumpster!

Finally, she did manage to ask some of her questions, but then thought, "does it really matter if I get my questions answered? Not really. I want to develop the beginnings of a relationship where I can feel free to contact him again. I'm not going to worry about the content of our discussion, but instead, just have a good talk."

They spent the rest of the 45 minutes in a full and open discussion. She ended up learning a lot about Frank and about Ronars even though some of her specific questions went unanswered. Frank asked her if she would call him in about 6 weeks as he anticipated some changes. He also asked for her resumé. He said he would send her some information about Ronars.

It had worked out well. The beginnings of a relationship were there. Jaya had achieved her main objective.

MAKING PERSONAL CONTACTS: THE INTERACTION

How do you open a discussion and engage another person in your opportunity search needs? Most people struggle with this issue. We want to leave a good impression. From the discussion we want suggestions of others to approach, or of employers who are looking for staff. We also hope the door will be open for a future contact.

We want more than a *transaction* with the other person; we want to develop a *relationship*.

Transaction: mechanical, lifeless, low personal interest, directed at getting our purposes achieved without regard for the other person. Our social interaction with the other person is to get in his or her good graces to get what we want. Many transactions are one-time discussions, with no interest on the part of either party in continuing them into the future.

Relationship: interactive, lively, high personal interest, directed at getting our purposes achieved, but with full respect for the other person and his or her needs and purposes. We seek to clarify our communication, to listen for what is said and the feeling behind the words, and to establish a contact that will go beyond this first meeting.

Telephone Contacts

The standard networking method – the one that has proven itself – is to phone people. You explain that you are seeking information or searching for a job. You would like to get some advice. You may point out that you are aware that there is little likelihood of an opportunity at the contact's firm at the moment. Being direct about this may ease the contact's mind and make it easier to gain the information you need.

At this point, you request an opportunity to meet briefly. You want to make yourself known and ask a few questions to assist you in your search. If the contact agrees, the balance of the encounter is played out at the meeting. If all goes well, you should be able to meet personally with about one-third of your contacts. If he or she will not agree to meet you, then you should do your best to obtain as much pertinent information as you can over the telephone.

Knowing the direct telephone number of your contact helps in getting through. These days we often encounter voicemail. Usually by pressing "0" or the pound key (#), you will default to a receptionist. She may be able to locate the person you want to speak with, or take a message, or tell you the best time to reach him or her. It is important to use the person's direct line. If you called a general information number, the receptionist who answers will usually give this to you.

Make every effort to talk directly with the person rather than leaving a message. Once you have the direct extension, call at times when voicemail is not likely being used. These times would be, typically, in the morning before 8 a.m., during the lunch hour, and after 4:30 p.m. If you encounter voicemail, hang up and do not leave a message.

If you have not been able to reach the person in three or four tries, then leave a message on voicemail. Here are some rules of thumb for leaving a message:

- Have an organized, focused message. Prepare and rehearse it in advance. Read it if this helps you to sound more organized.

- Give the essential information (who, why, number). Keep the message to less than 30 seconds.

- Start by saying your name and giving the purpose of your call.

- Sound friendly. It helps to smile while talking on the telephone.

- Use the name of an intermediary whenever possible. "'X' suggested I call."

- Speak clearly and slowly. Your name and phone number should be especially clear. Remove all verbal twitches such as "uh."

- Repeat your name and phone number. Your message should end with a thank you. Say that you're easy to reach and indicate how.

- If an edit feature is available on the person's voicemail, use it. If you are not happy with your message, erase it and try again. If you have a friend with editable voicemail, seek permission to practice on her line.

In case you successfully reach the person, have a plan in front of you as to the purpose of your call, some questions you would like answers to, or some proposed times and dates for a personal, in-office meeting. The actual hiring of employees results from meetings between applicant and hirer and very rarely over the telephone.

Script the first sentence of your call.

If the respondent answers the phone and identifies herself, you could respond as follows:

"Hello, this is Mike Smith. I don't believe we have met before. I am presently carrying out a career search. With your background and experience (in . . . ., or as a . . . .), I thought (or someone suggested) you could be helpful to me. Could we meet for 20 minutes in your office? This would give me a chance to describe my objectives and to hear any suggestions or advice you might have. I have time to meet tomorrow at almost any time, or on Friday morning."

As you attempt to find out what is available, your need may be for an informational meeting. In this case the emphasis is on research rather than presenting yourself as a candidate for a job. You are attempting to find out about an industry sector or to pursue a new career. Your request is to meet the knowledgeable contact to get answers to some key questions.

Whether networking or researching, you will get one of the following four responses or variations. You can prepare in advance for them.

Script #1 Phone respondent – *"No, I can't meet you, and in fact I am busy now and can't talk to you."*

Your response: Ask first if you could call back later, and when you could call. If this is achieved, then terminate the call.

If this is not achieved, ask if you could send your resumé. "Could I send you my resumé in case you have suggestions or want to keep it on file?" Whatever the response, this is the time to conclude the contact.

Script #2 Phone respondent – *No, I can't meet you, perhaps I can answer your questions now?"*

Your response: Be prepared with specific questions you would have asked in a personal interview. Explain your area of competence briefly. Ask for views on the job market in general, knowledge of any organizations where there are openings, and the names of other people to contact. Depending on your evaluation of the quality of the contact, you might ask for permission to use the contact's name in calls to the suggested referrals.

Ask if you can send a resumé. With your resumé, include a thank-you note both for the information and the time spent by the contact in talking to you.

In a first contact don't explain why you plan to leave or have left your previous employer unless it is specifically asked for. If you must explain, outline the reasons but leave out any anger or other emotions that you may honestly feel about leaving. Be objective, straightforward and brief. Too much emotional honesty in this first contact may receive a sympathetic hearing, but actually turn off the receiver and hurt your chances for further contact.

Sometimes opportunities arise where you can help the person you are calling. This might take the form of information or knowledge of value to your contact. Reciprocity strengthens the quality of your contact.

Script #3 Phone respondent – *"Tell me more about your situation and why you want to meet me."*

This person probably wants to refuse an interview but either has difficulty saying no, or has a genuine curiosity from what you have said so far. Sometimes this response comes from someone who actually has a suitable job available but does not want you to know it.

The trap for the job searcher is going into so much detail over the phone that a personal interview seems unnecessary.

Provide enough information to pique interest without telling your whole story. You continue to strive to obtain a personal meeting.

Your response: "I am a xxx professional and have more than a decade of experience. My work life has taken me into some very interesting situations and, since you are in my field (familiar with my field), I am sure you will have heard about some of them. My basic objectives in personally meeting with you include getting acquainted with you, telling you a little of my background and getting your advice on the market for the professional services I offer. I won't take more than 20 minutes of your time."

If you are unsuccessful in getting an interview, treat the call as if it were a #2.

Script #4 Phone respondent – "I would be happy to meet with you if we can find a mutually satisfactory time."

Your response: you simply arrange for a convenient time and reassure the contact that you won't overstay your welcome.

Interview timing

If you establish a specific length of time for your networking interview, make sure you honor this commitment. If you established 20 minutes as the time, then when 20 minutes have passed, you should acknowledge it by saying, " I said I would only take 20 minutes of your time, and 20 minutes have passed. I would like to thank you for your assistance." At this point you will judge the quality of your interaction and decide whether to ask if you can keep in touch, send a resumé or use the name of the interviewer in contacting referrals.

Only stay past the deadline if the person you are interviewing specifically requests that you stay. If you stay, continue to be conscious of the time. The interviewer has not opened the door for a two-hour session! A total of 45 minutes should, in almost all situations, be the outside time of an interview. That is, the 20 minutes you requested plus another 25 minutes at the request of the interviewer.

Networking For Jobs

The process of networking has proven to be the most powerful means of locating and obtaining jobs. Between 60 and 80 percent of new opportunities are found in this way. How does it work? The first section of this chapter identified what to say. Now we will concentrate on other factors.

Networking lets you identify potential positions through other people. These may be people you know or they may be completely unknown to you. You should not restrict your contacts exclusively to those you know.

Meeting face-to-face is important for a number of reasons:

- More time is available for discussion. Instead of a five or ten minute phone conversation, you may have 20 to 45 minutes in the contact's office.

- You will get more information in a face-to-face discussion. Ideas will occur to your contact that might not otherwise have surfaced.

- You can demonstrate your competence and interpersonal skill in this brief discussion.

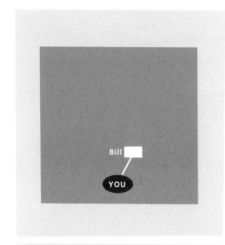

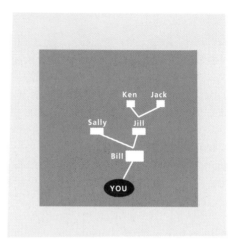

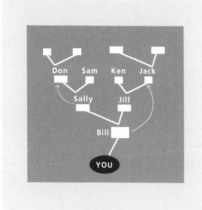

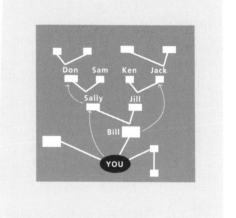

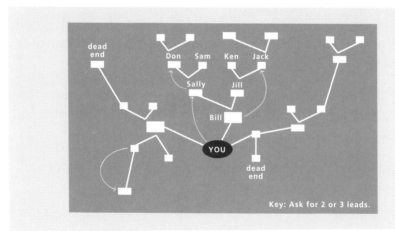

Key: Ask for 2 or 3 leads.

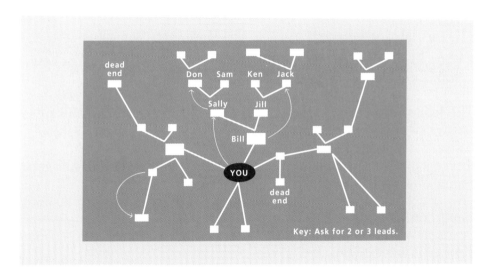

- If the meeting was a good one, you are much more likely to be remembered. You may be referred to a viable lead or even to a job because you left a favourable impression.

Your initial goal is to obtain information. Unless you know for certainty of an available position, stay away from selling yourself for a job with your contact's firm. This will only turn your contact into a negative one, particularly if you said all you wanted was advice.

What advice and information do you need?

Here are some of the questions you might ask your contact:

- Would he or she be aware of openings in your field?

- Are there larger changes expected in the industry likely to result in positions being available?

- From the contact's perspective, what are the prospects like in your field?

- Can the contact suggest the names of other people you could talk to?

The last question is vital. It is the key to networking. You need names of new contacts so that you can keep your network alive.

There will always be a number of contacts who can offer you good ideas and who know about jobs. From time to time, you may encounter a contact at whose firm there is an opening that is being kept confidential. If you present yourself well, you may find yourself on the inside track to a job that has not yet been, or may never be, advertised.

Important elements in networking.

- Make many contacts, both by phone and in person. One or two a day is not enough. See Chapter 4, The Job Search Schedule.

- Be clear. Don't leave your contacts guessing about your area of expertise.

- Observe normal courtesies. Be pleasant, gracious, and interested in your contact.

- Be positive and upbeat. People who exude doom and gloom are not well-received.

- Follow up on the contact by letter or phone. Thank him or her for the interview and the help offered. This will also serve to further remind the contact of your availability.

Networking is extremely important, yet many job searchers find it one of the most difficult job search activities. This results mainly from our fears, anxieties and hesitations concerning how others will respond to us. Remind yourself that your anxieties come from *your* view of the world, and have no connection to how you will actually be treated. If you are courteous, clear in your objectives and gracious with the other person, he or she will usually reciprocate in kind.

REACHING PEOPLE WHO ADVERTISE JOBS

Most job searchers respond to advertised positions. In perhaps 15 to 25 percent of cases, job searchers locate their future employer in this way. However, you have to make your application stand out in some way, since dozens or even hundreds of people will usually apply to attractively advertised jobs. Here are some ways you can give yourself "an edge" when you reply to ads:

- *Read the ad carefully,* factoring out all the requested candidate attributes.

- *Reply to the ad in specific terms.* If you include a resumé, and this is not always the thing to do, make sure it is specifically tailored to *this* ad.

- *Always include a covering letter addressed to a person.* This may require you to contact the company to find out the name of the "Personnel Officer," or the person with a similar title. Use the normal last name salutation, e.g., Dear Mr. (or Ms.) ___.

- *Even if requested, it is not usually a good idea to include references or salary requirements.* You might write, "In a subsequent discussion I will be pleased to supply references," or "My salary requirements are flexible, in line with the responsibilities of the advertised position." Or you might just leave out any response to the references and salary questions. If you have the skill and experience required, the absence of this information will not normally cause you to be eliminated from the competition. Remember: the company's objective is to find ways to screen people out so that only a handful need to be interviewed. Every aspect of your response to an advertised position will be evaluated with this goal in mind. If your resumé indicates a salary expectation that is much higher or lower than what the organization has established as a benchmark, you may never get the interview strictly based on your stated salary requirements.

- *If possible, get more information about the job* by contacting the company before sending your response. You can then add to your resumé or cover letter items addressing aspects of the job that were not mentioned in the advertisement. Telephoning the company also provides you with an opportunity to present yourself, which, if carried off well, may help you to get an interview. When organizations specifically indicate in their ad that they don't want phone calls, this must be observed.

- *Send fresh copies of your resumé.* Tired, worn-out, dog-eared resumés are rarely taken seriously.

- If your experience is not a good fit with the job requirements, *send only a letter* (even if a resumé is requested). In this letter, you should set out the attributes and experience you do have that would make you successful in the job. Including a resumé outlining your marginal experience is likely to rule you out of the competition. As well, if you can devise other means of meeting the organization's representatives which do not involve a written response, and they are favorably impressed, this will go a long way towards offsetting any deficiencies in your actual work experience.

- *Wait a few days*, even a week, before responding to ads placed by *larger* organizations. This might seem counterproductive.

However, the first replies to a large competition end up on the bottom of the pile and can be eclipsed by the more recent replies in the mind of the person reading them. Later replies can sometimes have a significant advantage.

- *Respond immediately to smaller organizations.* Smaller companies may be considering candidates, interviewing some and ruling out others, as responses arrive. In such cases, an immediate response may be crucial. In fact, smaller companies will sometimes be pleased if you seek an opportunity to personally bring in your resumé and have a brief initial interview on the spot.

- *Follow up on your ad response* approximately two weeks after you sent it in to ensure it arrived and to find out how the sorting process is advancing. By following up, you can also restate your strong interest and desire for an interview.

Looking for a job exclusively by responding to ads may be discouraging and delay your re-employment. It is crucial to go after jobs available through the "hidden job market" where, for a variety of reasons, available positions are not being advertised. See Chapter 4, The Job Search Schedule, for a section on persistence of contact.

RECRUITERS AND PLACEMENT AGENCIES

Many job searchers think immediately of "head-hunting" firms to solve their unemployment problem. These firms are in the business of assisting organizations to find suitable candidates for vacant or soon-to-be-vacant positions. Here are some important factors to consider when contacting recruiters or placement agencies.

First of all, there are generally two types of recruiters, the executive search firm and the placement agency. It is sometimes difficult to distinguish between these two general categories, and some firms do both types of work.

The executive recruiter has an exclusive relationship with an organization to find candidates for a position. The recruiter is either paid for the time put into the search or on a retainer basis, some or all of which will be paid even if the search is not successful. The recruiter, sometimes called an executive search consultant, wants to find someone who fits the position well, and in so doing, gets repeat business. Usually the recruiter identifies three or more suitable candidates for consideration by the client – the retaining organization. Organizations use executive recruiters to assist them in filling their more senior management and professional positions.

Placement agencies receive a finder's fee. They usually have assignments to find technical and front-line people. They are paid when someone they recommend actually starts in the position and often compete with other placement agencies attempting to fill the same position. In general, a placement agency will put more of an onus on the company to decide the fit. They will put their energies into finding qualified candidates.

Always ask placement agencies to advise you first, before they send your resumé to their client firms. Without this request, some agencies may just send your resumé to a number of firms hoping it will be considered. This may hurt your hiring chances if you have already contacted one of these firms. They may not appreciate being subject to an agency fee for someone who has already contacted them.

Don't hesitate to contact agencies. It is illegal for them to charge you a fee for any contact, and they do need candidates for jobs. Phone to make an appointment. Or write first, then phone. These agencies are usually very small, with a handful of consultants. They can be quite entrepreneurial and marketing oriented, and in general, very responsive to anyone who is taking initiative and making contacts. They fully understand the job search process.

The same personal contacting principles apply when contacting agencies. In this case, however, remember that agencies are in the business of identifying people for jobs. Their client is the organization, not you. If they have nothing in your field, they are unlikely to want to see you, or even spend much time with you on the phone. When they do agree to meet you, there is a good chance they currently hope to identify candidates like you, even though they may deny it or play it down. You must take very seriously any opportunity to meet with a recruiter.

If you make an exceptionally good connection with a recruiter who encourages you to keep in touch, make a point of calling every four to six weeks to let him or her know you are still available. But be careful! If you have not established a good relationship with the recruiter, these frequent calls may be regarded as an annoyance and do more harm than good.

If you successfully get to see someone from an agency, or even if you can manage to have a good phone conversation with him or her, you will get job searching information. These people are out and around, doing their own marketing. They hear about changes and companies that are adding staff. Even if they don't have an assignment to find someone like you, they may know of organizations that are hiring people with your qualifications.

Reply to all recruiter-placed ads where you qualify. Even if you feel you have excellent qualifications, you may not even make the short list. Frequently, unspoken qualifications will rule you out. This may seem unreasonable, but it is reality.

Recruiters are notorious for not getting back to people when they say they will. Accept this as a fact of life. It is not a personal slight. If a recruiter indicates he or she will be calling back on a certain day and fails to do so, leave it for two or three more days and then call. You can ask, "How is your search coming?", "Am I still in the running?", "Is there some area of my expertise on which you would like me to elaborate?" and so on.

Finally, recruiters and placement agencies represent a very small part of the overall market for job openings. We estimate that about 10 percent of job searchers find positions through them. But as mentioned above, they are excellent sources of information. They need you. And you *could* be the "one in ten" selected for a new position through a recruiter or a placement agency.

QUESTIONS AND ANSWERS

- *What can you do when calls are not returned?*

The short answer is "move on." A certain percentage of people will not return your calls. Consider it as part of the "numbers game." In order to get a response from 10 people, you likely need to call 15. Five you will never hear from. If you brood over the un-returned calls, you will just upset yourself unnecessarily. The person you have tried to reach may be away, ill, too busy, or he or she may just not answer calls from mystery people. Whatever the reason, after you have called, perhaps tried several times, and left a voice mail without result, give it up and go on to others.

- *What are some great opening sentences for cold calls?*

Not, "How are you today." You are not a telemarketer.

Try, "My name is xxxxx and I am presently on a search for a new position. Right now, I am networking, ...making contacts to identify information that will help me in my search. I was wondering if there is any chance we could meet briefly so I could get the benefit of your thoughts?"

"This is yyyy, and I am wondering if I could have 20 minutes of your time in your office sometime this next week? I am on a career search, and networking. Your name came up as a person who could give me some good advice. Are you free, for example, for a few minutes on Thursday afternoon?"

• *How do I decide which agencies to contact?*

Many search firms or placement agencies do have specialties. Get a listing of them. There is a directory of these firms, which you can find at the public library. Some directories have annotations, which identify their special areas of interest. Otherwise, get the list and phone the receptionist at each firm and ask if the firm has a specialty. Contact those firms that specialize in placing people in your profession. Contact all the firms that indicate they work as generalists. It is better to use many search firms and placement agencies. There is no advantage in using only a few.

• *Do I have any obligations to placement agencies or search firms, once contacted?*

They have no obligation to you, nor you to them. The client is the organization that is searching for someone. The search firm is on the lookout for appropriate candidates and is not representing you simply because you contacted them or sent them your resumé.

• *What are effective ways of using search firms and placement agencies?*

Get information from them. They are well-connected in the community as a result of their own marketing efforts. If they have a job available that fits your capabilities put yourself forward as favorably as possible. Getting an interview with the recruiter may be the only route to some positions.

- *Do I need to inform the search firms and placement agencies I originally contacted once I have found a new position?*

These firms will not expect you to contact them. However, if you are in the middle of discussions with a recruiting firm, and accept a position through another source, it would be appropriate to advise the recruiter. Also, if you have made excellent personal contacts in agencies, it would be courteous to write or phone them to advise that you have taken a position. They may remember this when you have a future need for a position, or apply to them in connection with another listing they are representing.

- *How do you follow up on networking contacts?*

If you establish a good contact, ask if you can maintain contact with him or her. Call the contact periodically to tell him/her how you are doing on your search. Be cautious to not overdo these contacts. Send the contact interesting industry information. Always ensure you thank contacts verbally and through the mail for their assistance and friendship.

- *How do you deal with a situation where the person you have set up a meeting with does not show up, or leaves a message that he or she can't meet you after all?*

Many people are absolutely thrown off balance by this situation. But people who are in direct sales know that it is a common occurrence. Don't obsess over an apparent slight. There may be some very good reasons why the person has not turned up, or has indicated she can't see you. It usually has nothing to do with you.

Assume the best, and call the person again to attempt to set up another time to meet.

- *How do you promote yourself when you have 30 seconds, on an elevator, for example?*

Usually what happens is that you meet someone you have known from the past and you realize that that person could be a good contact for you in the course of your search. Be very direct; get right to the point. Don't try to do anything more than set up something for the future.

After the initial greeting, say, "I'd like to give you a call – do you have a card?" or "I'd like to talk to you – who are you with now? ………. I'll be in touch in a day or two."

- *How do you establish contacts when your main focus is on a marketplace in a distant city?*

Searching is not easy when it requires long distance calls or four-hour plane trips. If you have an unlimited budget you can call people in the same way that you would call in your local area. Call people you know, or call cold to names pulled out of directories. In advance, establish a two-week period when you plan to visit, and set up meeting dates for that time period.

Responding to ads can pay off. The hiring firm is sometimes carrying out an international search and hopes to draw in candidates from any and all locations. Unfortunately the competition is usually stiff.

This is where the Internet may be valuable. Many jobs open to people on a broad basis are advertised on the Job Board sites on the 'Net. This can be an excellent way of identifying real opportunities in a location far away from your home base.[7]

- *Should I phone hiring firms that state in their advertisement that resumés are to be sent but no phone calls are to be made?*

It is best to adhere to their wishes.

---

[7] For Canadian websites for job searchers, go to www.garthtoombs.com and follow the links to "Helpful Websites."

INTERVIEWS

"I'll just wing it," Joan said to her husband, as she left the house for the interview of her life. She was qualified for the job. She wanted this job. She could already feel herself in the position carrying out changes and making improvements.

Although she knew that at least six others were being considered, she had done little to prepare for this interview.

She thought, "I know the area, I know this company, I know my abilities, why should I prepare? And, anyway, how can you prepare to be interviewed for a job? You never know what they are going to ask."

She arrived quite a bit early at the office of Durald & Deming and spoke to the receptionist who asked her to take a seat in the waiting room. There was another woman in the chair across from her. She assumed that she was likely there for an interview as well. Joan noticed how well dressed her competitor was. She had on a nicely tailored suit, appropriate accessories and shoes that were a perfect fit for her outfit.   Joan realized that she had not given much attention to what she was wearing. It had never crossed her mind. She had put on the same skirt and blouse she had worn to the office dozens of times before.

Someone came to get her competitor for the interview. As they left the waiting room she noticed how easily the two engaged in conversation, led by her competitor.

About 30 minutes later the competitor emerged, talking to the interviewer in an easy and animated fashion. There was a further exchange of pleasantries, and she was gone.

Joan was soon sitting in the room with Ms. Brown and Mr. Walls. Mr. Walls started right in with a question that threw Joan for a loop. He said, "Tell us a little about yourself."

Joan became defensive: "But, what exactly do you want to know?"

Mr. Walls looked a little uncomfortable at having to explain. "I just want you to tell us something about yourself that you think is important so we can get a general impression of you."

Joan swallowed. "Well there's so much to tell. Let me see ... I can tell you about my educational background ... How long do I have?"

And so, the interview went from bad to worse because Joan had not prepared for it. The impression she made by her appearance and by the answer to the first question was not good. She was well-qualified for the job, but didn't get it.

WHAT TO EXPECT; HOW TO ACT

Companies almost always interview more than one candidate for a position. Sometimes the interview is concurrent with the decision. In such a situation, a decision follows each interview: the candidate is either hired or ruled out. If he or she is hired, the interview process stops. If not, the next candidate is considered and another decision made, and so on, until someone has been hired. For the well-prepared candidate, this is a favourable situation.

Normally, though, the company will interview several candidates and consider all of them before making a decision. In this process, the last candidate interviewed usually has a slight advantage because of the "recency'" effect. A candidate who has been more recently interviewed will be remembered better, and if equally qualified with other aspirants, may get the nod for the job.

Research and Preparation

Getting prepared for a job interview may take several hours. Here are some ways successful job searchers prepare for interviews:

- *Research the organization.* Go to the library for annual reports, news reports and financial records. Talk to people presently employed by the organization to find out what they think and know about it. What are some of the current concerns and issues? Does it have stated short and long term objectives? Talk to the company's suppliers – what have they observed and experienced?

- *Find out what you can about the person or people who will interview you.* How long have they been with the organization? Where did they come from? What are their attitudes towards the organization?

- *Does high turnover cause you to wonder what some of the organization's problems are?* Is there burnout, excessive stress or workaholism? Do people have interests outside of their work?

- *Prepare for questions that might be asked.* Acquire a standard set of questions and get someone to ask you these questions. Critique your answers, the length of your answers (they should be short), and think especially carefully through answers to "touchy" questions such as "Why are you no longer with ABC company?" or "What are your salary expectations?" or "What is your major shortcoming?"

- *Thoroughly review your work history.* Recall specific projects and the success (or lack of it) you had with them. What did you like and dislike about certain positions? Why did you leave previous employers? What difference did your presence make to previous organizations? What added value do you bring to a future employer?

Many organizations now use targeted, or "behaviour description techniques," to frame questions to applicants. These questions assume that you will probably repeat in any future job your actual behaviour in your last or current job. This means that the interviewer may probe to discover very specific examples of your past behaviour and results. A general answer will not do. For example, you might be asked, "Tell me about a time in the past when you successfully completed a difficult task. What was the task? What was the outcome? Be specific. I want descriptions, times, dates, people involved."

INTERVIEW TIPS

Once you have been invited to a job interview, you are in a position to achieve your goal of being employed again. This will probably be a competitive situation where others are also being considered.

You may not be certain that the job is right for you. Whatever the situation, however, you want to put your best foot forward. You want to be the best you can be, to land a job offer. If it's not right for you, you can always turn it down. But there may be other options as well – for example you might be able to have some changes made to the job specifications that will make it better suited to your interests and abilities.

Take into consideration the following points when you finally meet the interviewer(s) face-to-face.

- *"Affect" will influence whether or not you are hired just as powerfully as the information you provide.* Be upbeat, friendly, positive, enthusiastic and interested.

- *Everyone you see can have an influence* when you go for your interview. Be pleasant to administrators, receptionists, mail clerks and anyone else you come in contact with prior to, or after the interview. Any of these people may be asked to comment on you.

- *The first few seconds and minutes are very important in an interview.* This includes the exchange of greetings, the handshake, and the pleasantries as you go to the office or interview area. Be prepared for this exchange by how you dress, your tone of voice, your posture, hair, shoes, etc. These first moments result in an initial impression. If positive, you are already one step further along the road to obtaining the position.

- *The first question in an interview is often a general one.* "Tell me about yourself" is one form of this type of question. Don't reply with a defensive "Well, what do you want to know?" Be prepared to review briefly some of the key items in your work history. Relating a relevant achievement can be impressive at this point.

- *Keep your replies brief and to the point.* One test of the length of reply is whether your interviewer could fully summarize your response easily. If you go on too long, this will not be possible.

- *Conversational interviews serve the interviewee well.* You ask about the organization, its progress and plans, as well as answering the interviewer's questions. As a result, the interviewer will take a much greater interest in you. This is not always possible in highly structured situations where the interviewer has a list of questions to ask.

- *Especially, at first, stay away from issues related to compensation.* Early in an interview you may rule yourself out by revealing a salary requirement far above or below what the job offers. After the interviewer, and perhaps others in the company, have come to know you and determine that they want you, compensation becomes a topic of negotiation rather than a reason not to hire you. Read Chapter 12 on Negotiating Compensation.

- *Final impressions* are also very important, and you should have one or two closing questions that convey intelligence, interest and enthusiasm.

- *Follow up the interview with a thank-you letter* affirming your interest in the position (if indeed you are interested). Where candidates are considered equal, a well-written thank you note may tip the balance.

Eleven Common Questions

- Tell me about yourself.
- Why do you want to leave your present job, or why did you leave your last job?

- What do you see as your major strengths?

- What do you see as your major weaknesses?

- What are the most difficult problems (situations) you have faced in your most recent job? How did you deal with them?

- What do you consider your greatest achievement?

- What is your long-range career goal?

- What do you dislike about your present or last job?

- Why would you say you are effective in working with (or managing) other people?

- What would you prefer not to have to do in your next job?

- What are your compensation requirements?

Interviewers list questions reflecting their beliefs, values or interests. Some questions will explore your competence to carry out the technical components of the job. Other questions determine past experiences that would demonstrate a high level of competence in an area related to this job. Review possible questions. Write them out ahead of time and consider your responses. What do you want to communicate to the interviewer? Ensure that you make these points, as appropriate, during the interview.

DRESS AND DEPORTMENT AT THE INTERVIEW

What you wear and how you behave make a very clear statement. Interviewers and even job search contacts will certainly notice this statement even though the discussion may focus on your knowledge, skill and past achievements. In fact, things not discussed – your mannerisms, verbal expressions, or clothing, for example – can be just as important as the quality of your replies in deciding to remove you from consideration.

Clothing

A number of years ago, two of us were interviewing a young man for a fairly senior role in a large organization. He was well-dressed and was wearing the latest in the way of shoes for that time, but they were dark blue in color. We completed the interview, which he handled extremely well. After he had left, my co-interviewer made only one disparaging comment: "but can you imagine him in front of our department with blue shoes on?" He was dropped without another comment because we knew that some would not take him seriously because of those blue shoes. We had several other good candidates and there was no need to consider him further.

This may seem like an extreme example, but it makes the point that how you dress is extremely important. Men should wear conservative clothes to an interview, while dressing slightly upscale in relation to the people in the organization. Don't wear anything that might draw particular attention to itself, such as a gaudy tie . . . or blue shoes!

Women should also dress conservatively. A short skirt combined with a deep chair can leave many women self-consciously tugging at their hemlines. Women have several options. A conservative skirt, or slacks and jacket convey a better message.

Perfume can also cause problems. There are few perfumes that someone doesn't find offensive and you might be in front of an interviewer who, unbeknownst to you, does not like your particular brand of perfume. Or worse – he or she might be allergic to perfume.

Today many work settings don't require that people wear jackets or ties. Many people come to work in jeans and very casual tops. Should the person being interviewed be equally casual?

In many settings it will be appropriate for men to come without ties. Women can also dress more casually than in the past. In field locations, dress can even be a step more casual.

But you want to be careful. Check out the "dress code" by asking the interviewer what the normal workplace requires. Or, ask someone who works there. Then, dress upscale from what you have been told. It is always better, and makes a more positive statement, when you come to interviews dressed carefully and appropriately to the setting.

Behaviour

Are there any behaviours to avoid? There are many. Being extremely familiar by using first names without being invited to, or taking the interviewer you have just met into your confidence regarding some personal or private matter, will be considered unprofessional.

The use of bad language and the telling of off-color or racist jokes are totally inappropriate. There are, however, other more subtle behaviours that will often hurt your chances. Talking too much or too fast is a common problem, as is the reverse – particularly if you answer in monosyllables, with little explanation or background, and the interviewer has to drag every bit of information out of you.

Here are some frequently seen bad interviewing habits which can keep you from being hired:

- *Constant use of bridging words* such as "and", "but," "you know" and "like"; overuse of meaningless expressions such as "and so on".

- *Constantly repeating an expression* similar to "you understand what I mean" gives the impression that the person being interviewed does not think very highly of the intelligence of the interviewer.

- *Poor eye contact* makes the interviewer feel like an object. The candidate appears to be addressing his or her answers to the walls, windows, paintings or desk.

- *A too-intense posture* such as sitting on the edge of the chair, leaning far forward, or a too-relaxed stance, sunk deep into the chair, leaning back.

- *Putting yourself down,* being negative or coming across as having little conviction.

- *Boring, monotone, or droning answers* can leave some interviewers feeling that the candidate should be on the market as a substitute for sleeping pills!

Many interviewers talk about a general feeling of discomfort concerning a person they have just interviewed. Often the reason for this relates to the area of dress and deportment. The candidate is qualified and answered the questions reasonably well, but there is *something else*, something indefinable, that has made the interviewer uncomfortable.

Prepare for the unspoken and less-visible part of the interview as well as for the discussion and questions that form the visible part.

QUESTIONS AND ANSWERS

- *How do you project confidence, enthusiasm, assertiveness, and energy during an interview?*

You need to feel these attributes to truly project them. People often build their confidence and energy by reviewing what they have done in their careers. They realize much has been accomplished. There is reason to be enthusiastic.

For practical feedback on how you project energy and assertiveness, practice using an audio or video tape recorder. Play back your responses. How energetic do you sound? How long were your answers? Were they clear? Do you have any bad habits?

Answer hypothetical questions in front of the mirror and observe such characteristics as your facial expressions, body language and smile.

To a considerable degree a problem in this area is a "thinking" problem. We know that we can upset ourselves and make ourselves sick by thinking negative thoughts or focusing on negative concerns. By the same token, it is possible to do the opposite. If we think about our achievements and successes, and the examples of our abilities, we will be much more confident, which will show through in the interview.

• *What is an unstructured interview and how do you deal with it?*

An unstructured interview can take many forms. It might be a "social" interview over dinner or at the golf course. It might be unstructured because the interviewer hasn't the slightest idea about what he or she will ask the person being interviewed.

The interviewee should take such interviews to be a great opportunity. He/She can ensure that key points are slipped in during the course of the unstructured discussions, as part of the discussion. "When I was at Harvard in '97...." gets across a key bit of information. "I really enjoyed leading the manufacturing team, and for the first time we broke the $100 million barrier...." presents a key accomplishment.

The interviewee should know in advance exactly what she/he wants the other person to hear, and simply ensure that all the points are made during this unstructured time.

• *How do you deal with negative questions in an interview?*

The interviewer might say, "I understand from my contacts that you miss a lot of work? Tell me about this."

Be honest. Is it true? If so, why do you miss work. Illness? Involvements in the community? Leaves of absence for lengthy vacations? The interviewer essentially wants you to know that he/she knows about this, and to be reassured that it won't be repeated in the future.

Leave the interviewer on a positive note when concluding the answer to a negative question. "I did miss work with the company's blessing while I was working on the United Way Campaign, but this involvement is over. I would not take on volunteer commitments which take me away from work as I found it led to misunderstandings, even though I was always able to complete my work."

• *How do you handle inappropriate or illegal questions?*

If you don't mind answering a question about your age, family situation, children, health, religion or ethnic background, then simply answer it. However, if you don't want to respond, or feel it will put you at a disadvantage, or if you feel it is intrusive, and know it's illegal, but you want the job, then consider carefully how you will respond.

"Does this have a bearing on the position? Tell me how it does, and I will certainly answer it fully." This response, if well presented, usually will not offend the interviewer, but it will cause him/her to back off on the question itself.

- *How do you handle questions about gaps in employment or the gap since you were last employed?*

People often try to fudge over these gaps or hope they won't be asked about them. If it's a gap since you were last in a job it might be simply explained by saying you have been on an "all out" job search, and that these things take time. It is true that some people take up to a year or more to find the right job.

Most people, including interviewers, have experiences, personally or with their family or friends, where there have been protracted periods of absence from formal work settings. The reasons include illness, raising a family, or taking time off to get revitalized or refocused in a career. Sometimes it just looks like a person has a gap in their employment, when, in fact, they were involved in full-time study, or contract work.

Don't assume that the interviewer would automatically be negative about gaps. She may have a significant gap in her own formal work history. Explain your situation honestly and make sure the interviewer has the information about your qualifications for the job. The gap itself is unlikely to be a job breaker.

- *How do you handle overly talkative interviewers?*

One possibility to consider: that the overly talkative interviewer has already made up his mind to hire another candidate. Out of courtesy he is just going through the motions.

These behaviours, however, usually come from unskilled or new interviewers. Nervous and fearful of silence, they worry that you will be unimpressed with their knowledge or ability. In response, they talk too much. As an interviewee you should listen. You may gain insight about the position or organization that you can use in the interview.

Deal with this as you would deal with an unstructured interview. Get your information across, one way or another, to the interviewer. Take advantage of openings. Reduce the number of questions you ask because that just gives this interviewer, with the verbal diarrhea, a greater chance to explode with more talk.

Does such an interviewer listen anyway? Probably not well. See if you can meet with other people in the organization to ensure that they know you and your skills.

- *Is there a different strategy if a panel is interviewing you?*

Usually each panel member will be asking questions from a different perspective. The interview will be very structured. The applicant needs to identify the decision-makers and the person that he/she will be reporting to. Try to remember everyone's name. If they give you their cards, keep these in front of you.

Make eye contact with everyone as you answer the questions, but be especially sure to make eye contact with your potential supervisor. He may not necessarily be the most vocal person.

- *How do you discuss skills that are not objectively provable?*

One will experience difficulty quantifying such skills as "a good communicator," or "team-builder." Rather than making claims to being effective in "soft" areas, give examples. If you actually initiated and headed a team and the results of their work can be shown, this will go along way to proving you are a team-builder.

You can also attribute your "soft" skills to a third party (if it is true) by saying, "The head of our department told me on several occasions that I was a good team player."

- *How do I get my message across when the interviewer is from H.R. and I am a real "techie"?*

Like ships in the night, sometimes our messages don't get through to the very person we want to get to know and influence. Some people's thoughts take them to ideas, concepts and strategies while others are absorbed in physical structures, building materials and tools. Words can mean different things. Often interests don't connect.

People tend to hire people like themselves. Sometimes it's impossible for a "very different" person to break through that barrier. Acknowledging that there might be differences because of such varied backgrounds would be one way of dealing with the issue. If you are being interviewed, and you sense this potential minefield in your attempts to get the job, you could ask questions that would help you understand where this other person is coming from.

For example, you could say, "I expect when you look at the issue of planning, you are thinking about planning that involves people?" This might get you a response or partial response that then helps in the subsequent discussion.

- *How can you get feedback from completed interviews?*

Following an interview, people often want to know how they did and how they came across to the interviewers. Don't seek feedback on the spot. You might put the interviewers on the defensive. You may get a positive response, but only because they don't know how to tell you about some bad habit, or that you talked to much, or that you simply are not a fit for what they want.

A better time to seek feedback is after the decision has been made. If you have not been hired, you could approach the interviewers by phone on the basis that you would like to know how you are doing in interviews, to benefit future interviews. The last thing you want is to put them on the defensive by implying that they made a mistake in not hiring you, or by asking directly why they didn't hire you. Prepare a few specific questions you can ask about your personal presentation skills or how you answered one or two of the main questions. Also remember, they may not recall the interview all that well, if they have hired someone else. Don't ask for, or expect too much.

- *Dealing with interviews that are "too comfortable."*

"I had a great interview. The recruiter was interested in me and I felt very at home in my discussions with him."

Some experienced interviewers are masters at making people feel very comfortable. They say all the right things, and ask general questions that allow people to respond from many points of view. This does not, however, necessarily mean you have the inside track. In fact, you may have relaxed too much and showed both the good and bad sides of your personality.

In a "comfortable" interview you should be on your guard. Make sure you are answering questions completely but that you are not droning on and on. Appreciate the attentiveness of the interviewer but keep in mind that this interviewer is evaluating you in the same way as any other, to make decisions as to which person fits the job best. Listen; provide the information that the interviewer needs; don't overstay your welcome.

- *Dealing with the "why" question. "Why do you want to work for our company?"*

Put the organization first by identifying that you are looking forward to adding value and by demonstrating how your skills are a good fit with their needs and will add strength. The last thing to mention, if presented at all, is what the experience will do for you by way of adding to your skills and experience.

- *What is it like to be interviewed by a search firm or recruiter?*

These interviews are like any other. Preparation is very important. The total impression you make will have an affect on whether or not they recommend you to their client.
Key things to remember:
- They have a great deal of experience in interviewing and know what they want to find out.
- Their client - the organization retaining them - has specified certain "musts" for acceptable candidates. They are on the lookout to see if you have these attributes.
- They know the client and its environment and they want to ensure you hold attitudes and beliefs that will make you an acceptable candidate.
- They will be courteous and may not be totally up-front with you regarding your chances of being considered. If they are not considering you, they will likely advise you by letter.

WHO CAN EMPLOYERS CALL?

Some applicants truly believe that the long list of notable references they have will somehow pull them through to another position. On their list they will identify the degrees, positions, and special attributes of the references. This, however, is not as impressive as you might think. It often has the opposite effect of giving the impression that the applicant is more interested in status and name-dropping than being concerned with the ability to do the job.

REFERENCES

Job searchers need to have references. These are people to whom you can refer potential employers for a comment on your character, qualities and past performance. There are several key points to remember about identifying and using references.

- Identify three to five people who will act as your references. The list should include your most recent supervisor as well as others who know you from a work setting.

- Personally ask each person to be a reference. Don't assume, on the basis of a past good relationship or friendship, that the person will automatically serve as a reference.

- Meet with each reference to review your career objectives and the strengths and weaknesses that have emerged from your self-assessment. This will help them think about what they can say about you. Leave each of them with a copy of your current resumé.

- Clarify with the reference why you left or are planning to leave your job so that the two of you will give a consistent message to prospective employers.

- Keep your references informed about your progress by phoning them every five or six weeks.

- Consider providing your key reference (your most recent supervisor) with a verbal reference guideline. The two of you can discuss and agree on its final content. This guideline can help your key reference when he or she receives calls from prospective employers, and will enable you to better know what is likely to be said about you. This guideline should include your strengths, a weak area, the reason you left or plan to leave your job, and a review of your key achievements. It should also include information on when you started with the organization, and the key positions you held while there.

References are generally checked by telephone. Written references are still used by more junior employees but rarely by professionals and managers. Few job searchers will send a written reference unless it is entirely positive, and employers know this. They will usually want to verbally question your references.

Provide the exact number of references the prospective employer requests.

Provide the names of references that match the needs of the potential employer.

Ensure that you choose references that can be reached for comment. For example, make sure they are not on vacation or on an international assignment.

If you are uncertain about the kind of reference you will get from a past employer, refer to this fact when providing the name, and suggest that the person call other references to get a more balanced view.

Prepare your references by calling them once you have given a prospective employer their names. Advise them of the job and how well it would fit you.

Some employers will not provide references as a matter of company policy. Find other people who will. Most employers will at least verify your years of employment and your title.

Reference checking is usually the last step in the hiring process. It is meant to confirm the positive view the employer already has of the prospect.

Many companies do not check references at all – *but don't count on it.* Be ready!

QUESTIONS AND ANSWERS

- *Should I list references on my resumé?*

No. If you must produce a list, have it as a separate list which can be provided if needed. Some organizations don't ask for references or check with them. If they don't need them, don't provide them.

If, after one or several interviews they ask you for the names of references, you have an advantage. Now you can provide just the names of people that you believe will give good, accurate and relevant information.

- *Do I include references when asked to do so in a newspaper ad?*

Generally no. You don't want the organization checking your references before talking to you. No one can represent you better than you can. Include a statement in your response to the newspaper ad that indicates your willingness to provide references once you have had an initial interview. Most organizations will understand your reluctance, and may also assume that you are searching on an anonymous basis, and don't want your existing organization to know that you are on the job market. If you fit for the position, the recruiting organization will not likely rule you out because you haven't included a list of references.

The one major exception to this rule relates to applying for academic positions at institutions of higher learning. They do expect you to include references with the first application, and may not consider you if references are not there.

- *What if contacts are made with people I have not used as references?*

This is always a danger. Is it ethically improper for recruiters to find out about you from people other than your official references? Opinions differ on this question. Regardless of the ethics, it's done all the time. If the recruiter knows someone at the organization of the applicant she has difficulty resisting the temptation to make a quick call.

You can ask the prospective employer whom they called to get information about you. If you have a concern about someone they contacted, provide them with another counterbalancing reference. You could also share with them that the person they contacted might not provide a balanced view of your capabilities. You can cite reasons.

• *Can I sue someone who is "badmouthing" me?*

It is extremely difficult to prove that someone has been giving you a poor reference. If you confront him or her, you will get a denial. There is no written reference to take to a lawyer. There are instances where applicants who are very concerned about this issue hire someone to get a reference on themselves from the suspect person. In most cases, it only proves that the applicant was wrong, or that the areas of criticism have some validity, and would not be actionable in a court of law.

9

ENTREPRENEURSHIP AS A CAREER OPTION

If jobs are not available in your field, how can you become gainfully employed? An increasing number of people look for job alternatives that don't necessarily include a return to a corporate environment. The predictions are that the employment future holds an increase in prospects for those who establish a business, work on their own, or have contractual relationships with companies.

Many of us feel that we are not well-suited to be entrepreneurs or to work in the uncertain world of contracts and consulting. Yet, ready or not, more of us will have to be employers even if our only employee is us! The workplace demands it.

WHAT CAN YOU DO?

It can be argued that consumer needs don't actually arise from the consumer. Some creative person, who believes a new product or service will make life more efficient or more enjoyable for others, promotes it. People didn't need automobiles until they saw what they could do. You can apply this to a myriad of products. It also applies to services. No one saw the need for many types of consulting until they were exposed to how a consultant could add value to the business.

Arising from your experience may be an idea for a product or service that you believe would benefit others. But you don't pursue it. Many people feel that their area of expertise already has an overload of creativity emerging from others who got there first. Don't be discouraged - new ideas are the fuel for even more new ideas and innovations. You can build on the success of others by creating a business to compete with them by providing additional service, a better quality product or targeting different buyers.

Some people believe they simply do not have what it takes to become an entrepreneur.

Twenty-five years ago, my ten-year-old son said to me, "Dad, why don't you have your own business? Why do you work for other people?"

I remember at the time being very definite in responding, "I will always be an employee!"

I had grown up in a home where entrepreneurship was never considered to be a potential work option. My brother and I were expected to have jobs and to perhaps rise up the managerial ranks, but certainly not in the uncertain world of business ownership. My father, an academic, was absorbed in teaching and research at a university.

What changed me? I did have several careers in quite different employment settings. I was always looking for new things to do and to learn. I proved myself as a manager and progressed to the equivalent of a vice president in a large government agency. Then I got into small business as the manager of a branch of a cross-

Canada firm. I was left alone to organize it the way I saw fit. I learned as an employee how a small business works. Then when the opportunity arose to be an owner, with others, of a start-up business, it seemed like a natural thing to do, though I recognized there were significant risks. I eventually became the sole owner of the business, which ultimately grew to a staff of 25 before I sold it to several of the senior employees. But I did have this great entrepreneurial experience for 10 years.

My stint in business ownership has given me experience-based opinions on what it takes to be successful. In my case, I believe it included financial backing in the early stages, actively and constantly selling to ensure that potential users of our service knew about it. That part never ended. Of most importance, the company provided excellent service. The key success attribute in my case, I believe, was an optimistic outlook – I always assumed that we would be successful.

Don't discount yourself as a potential entrepreneur too early in the process. Here is a step-by-step process for self-discovery.

1. Write out several ideas for selling your services or setting up a business, or to produce and sell a product.

2. Write out as many advantages and disadvantages that you can think of for each of your ideas.

3. Select the idea which seems to have the best prospects and focus on it. You may come back to other ideas later.

4. Talk to at least six people about this idea. What objections do they pose? What ideas do they have to improve on it? Do at least three of them agree with you that the idea is worth pursuing? Don't worry about someone stealing your idea. People pursue their own interests and don't have the time or energy to develop someone else's ideas.

5. Prepare three pages or more on your idea. Talk about what it is, whom it would interest, and who else is already doing it.

How long would it take you to get up and running? How will you finance it? Are you prepared to promote it every day? Does it require excellent relationship skills and how can you assure yourself that you have this key ability? Do you need others involved in order to be successful? How much money do you expect to initially earn weekly, monthly and annually? Five years from now, if you were successful, what would your business be like?

6. What is your fallback position if you throw yourself into your dream and it doesn't work out? Perhaps you will carry out a traditional job search or try out another idea or, if you are at a late stage in your career, step into volunteer and leisure time pursuits more fully.

7. Ultimately your plan should put you in the position of both having an impact (with your service or product) and of creating options for your life (by making money). If either one of these are not present as part of your plan, it is likely not viable as a business venture. But, maybe there's another idea worth exploring........

BACKGROUND

Over the last decade, there has been a noticeable shift in career choices towards the entrepreneurial option. There are a variety of reasons.

Unemployment

Some theorists and practitioners think that the tendency to seek entrepreneurial careers correlates positively with the great uncertainty and instability in "normal" workplaces. As more people become unemployed, the competition for existing jobs increases, and increasing numbers of people seek "non-job" alternatives. Many of the unemployed take their savings or severance and invest in a business as one way to remain in the world of work.

Baby Boomers

The baby boom generation provides a separate explanation. They are reaching their fifties at a time when many organizations are downsizing. Some of the characteristics of people in this category who have been asked to leave their organizations include:

- Recipients of relatively large severance packages, by virtue of length of service and age;

- Highly educated people with a broad experience base;

- Increasingly, dual income families; and

- Those demotivated by the failed promise of security in retirement.

More of the unemployed in this group choose an entrepreneurial option.

Lifestyle Choices

People hear the message that they must be in charge of their own careers. With downsizings, everyone has been affected by job loss, some directly, the rest indirectly. It is clear to workers, whether on the payroll or in transition, that, ultimately, organizations do not look after their employees. Individuals must do that for themselves. The shift from a paternalistic world to the "Me Inc." approach is sought after for its intrinsic value. People want to be in control; they want to make decisions to maximize their usefulness; they want to be the integral part of the communications and decision-making process.

ENTREPRENEURIAL OPTIONS

Generally, the entrepreneurial career changer seeks one of five objectives that relate to the motivation and level of risk the individual is willing to take.

1. Consultant (tactical)

Becoming a consultant is a tactical move for some whose real purpose is to get back onto an organization's payroll. This underlying, longer-term objective colours their efforts to look for lasting entrepreneurial/consulting work. To be successful as a consultant, even if you don't expect to have the role for long, does require **focusing on the customer; building relationships and remaining open to the possibilities** presented by people who want to retain you.

2. Franchises

In a similar vein, choosing to buy a franchise puts you halfway through the entrepreneurial door. It minimizes risk by purchasing an established system, and in most cases does not reward a person for further entrepreneurial creativity. In fact, some who fear ending up in a bureaucracy find some franchises very bureaucratic. The success of many franchises has evolved from the development of an excellent, tried-and-true way of conducting business. Franchisees are expected to follow the system. After all, you're **buying a piece of the success story, and you need to fit their mould**. As well, the best franchises are usually the most costly and require a certain level of wealth in order to provide the upfront funding. For many, this puts becoming the owner of a good franchise out of the question.

3. Buying a Business

Buying a business is somewhat like buying a franchise, except many purchasers of non-franchise businesses see ways to change the business and improve it. They purchase an up-and-running cash flow expecting to make it better. Of extreme importance, the purchaser must review every aspect of the business and its financial records to **ensure that the promised cash flow will continue** well into the future.

4. Consultant (strategic)

Few businesses can operate without assistance from many contractors or independents providing specialized services. The trend is for the organization to hire only those people who can carry out the core work. They farm out other functions. For example, many organizations retain external consultants for anything and everything to do with computers, systems, web sites, local area networks, and to oversee their telecommunications systems. When it comes to marketing, external individuals are often used for advice and to do the conceptual thinking about corporate materials and approach to the marketplace. Some firms are now retaining a specialized external person to be their human resources manager. Even those employees who work in the core areas of the organization may retain other highly specialized, external people to assist them with special problems or at critical times.

A huge industry has developed to provide advice in the so-called "soft" areas of organization functioning and management. Many of these consultants working out of their homes find contracts and consulting work with a small number of organizations. Some consultants have banded together under a banner name. They still generate their own customers, but benefit from the advice and leads of other consultants in the group.

An external consultant achieves success because **he or she knows more about a certain area than anyone in the organization**. If people on the inside become capable in this area, then they no longer need the consultant. The major task for strategic consultants is to keep deepening or extending their knowledge so that organizations will continue to retain them.

Someone who aspires to be a strategic consultant needs **staying power** and an **ability to self-promote** without fear. Instead of searching for one job, the consultant is now on the lookout for a stream of opportunities. **Being clear about how you can make a contribution** and **not taking on too many different functions** appear to be keys to success for the entrepreneurial consultant. Of course, staying power is also important, as it may take many months or even a year or two before you see an income that comes anywhere near replacing what you were earning previously. Unfortunately, in this highly volatile area, many people are not successful and ultimately return to being employees.

5. Setting up a Business

Rather than buying a business, some entrepreneurs want to establish a business where they have a product or service to sell, and have facilities, inventory and employees.

If you grew up in a home where a parent owned a small business, you likely have an intuitive sense for how a business operates. You remember clerking in it. You remember your father or mother at the dining room table working on the company books. You remember the crisis that was caused when a particular supplier doubled his rates, or when a key employee fell ill.

People who have had this experience can understand the ebb and flow of a business better than those who dream of the idyllic life of being a small businessperson, but have not personally experienced it.

My grandfather came to the West at the age of 45 to homestead. He had never farmed in his life. He had owned and operated a hardware store in the East. He started with nothing but the land and the money he had from the sale of his business. He worked very hard, starting his farming business from nothing and raising a family with four children. His family joined him after a year, once he had erected a house and some buildings and had learned a great deal about farming. His youngest son learned to farm at his father's side, and became the next generation farmer, having developed the intuitive sense for what a farming business requires to be successful.

In today's world, a budding businessperson can take advantage of a great deal of advice. You can go to a bank, the government or private sources and you will get advice, or be given materials that will tell you to write up your idea, research it, find out about competition, and attempt to do an analysis of how much money it will take for start-up and for operations in the first two years.

About three out of four new businesses fail within the first five years of their existence. Because of this, it is very difficult to find financial institutions that will fund a newly starting business. There are some other sources, but a great many beginning entrepreneurs will borrow money from family members or friends, mortgage their homes, or use their savings or a severance to get started.

"Strategy precedes structure" may be the one truism in the infinite variety of paths that career change can take, especially for entrepreneurs. Step one is definitely NOT incorporation, or buying a computer, or creating business cards. Rather, start by developing a plan. What exactly is your service or product? Who will be your customers? How will you reach them? How will you price your service? What are your competitive advantages/disadvantages? What cash flow do you expect, and how does this fit for your cash demands? And so on. Once you have these questions worked out, structure is much easier.

ENTREPRENEURIAL ATTRIBUTES

What does an entrepreneur look like? How does he or she think or behave? It's worthwhile reflecting on some observations of common entrepreneurial attributes.

- Moderate level of risk taking. Entrepreneurs are not risk averse, yet they aren't foolish either. They seek a medium level of risk.

- Action orientation. Entrepreneurs do things.

- Add value. Entrepreneurs see ways to combine resources to add value, and be attractive to buyers. This is essentially how and why successful entrepreneurs make money.

- Persistence. Entrepreneurs don't go away.

- Self-reliance. Entrepreneurs have highly developed "bounce back" qualities. They also expect to "make it or break it" themselves.

- Family support. Family members are involved in all stages of getting the business up and running. They are totally "on side" in terms of the plan.

There are a number of career and psychological tests that can be helpful in providing a basis for the coaching of budding entrepreneurs.

TOOLS FOR ENTREPRENEURIAL VENTURES

A number of tools that could be helpful as a person develops his or her venture include:

- Personal assessment (various questionnaires are available)
- Business plans (essential for all business ventures – hard copy and software guides are readily available)
- Marketing brochures (multi-colour products are widely available in most locations)
- Consulting proposal
- Presentation overheads
- Presentation/marketing practice and training
- Business cards
- Special (one-on-one) legal advice
- Specialized software related to the kind of business venture
- Direct visits to businesses and franchises – "try one on for a day"
- Internet sites to advertise products and services

QUESTIONS AND ANSWERS

- *How easy is it to get business start-up funds from venture capitalists?*

Venture capitalists want to make a substantial rate of return on the investment of their funds. They are looking for ideas that will take off. New technologies, innovative services, ideas whose time has come are attractive to them. They require lots of documentation, but of very great importance is the confidence they feel in the entrepreneur. As a good first step, personally meet venture capitalists. Describe your idea. Listen to their questions. Get a feel for whether or not they will also "see the magic" of what you are proposing.

Venture capitalists like to assist people who are helping

themselves. They feel better about investing their funds if they can see that the entrepreneur also is going out on a limb financially.

The venture capital firm wants to own a piece of your business in return for its assistance. The firm wants to share in the potential and substantial upside. After all, the ultimate objective is to earn returns for investors. The firm may want more than a financial interest, and in some cases want to critically oversee your operation. Some firms of venture capitalists will have experts in finance, marketing and product development available to assist the businesses they have a stake in.

- *What are the most important traits of success for an entrepreneur?*

A lot of research has been done to answer this question. Even though some trends can be seen, there are always exceptions to the rule. Some people defy all the statistics and take their own advice, and become hugely successful. Most of us, however, should pay close attention to understanding what a successful entrepreneur is like, and attempt to follow in these footsteps.

Three attributes come immediately to mind. Successful entrepreneurs are pre-occupied with getting their business going. Everything else takes second place. They are action-oriented and not nearly as much into planning as some advisors would wish that they were. They have staying power. Their motivation to succeed in their business will last over several years, unabated.

- *How do you get started with a web-based business?*

There are tremendous opportunities to start businesses on the Internet. But this is a volatile area at the moment, and unless you already know something about what you want to do, and are personally amongst the elite in your understanding of the technology, it is probably not a good idea to attempt an Internet-based business. But, this does not stop you from working on understanding the Internet and attempting to identify niches and areas where you might be able to establish a business. Read books on the topic. Take a course, even if it is simply a day-long course in one aspect of the Internet. Talk to people who have already successfully established a web-based business. Surf the Internet to see if others have the same idea, to see how well they are doing.

- *How important is incorporation?*

You will need to connect with an accountant and possibly a lawyer on this issue.

If you operate as a consultant on your own, out of your home, we have heard that there is little advantage to incorporating. If you do incorporate, the government will require more extensive reporting. If you don't incorporate, you will still want to register the name of your business so that you can operate under it, with the assurance that no one else can legally use it.

You may want to incorporate for image enhancement. An incorporated business sounds more substantial.

There are many books and pamphlets that discuss this issue in detail, and professionals who can advise you. Governments also provide advice and sometimes financial support for prospective entrepreneurs.

- *How do you deal with ambivalence about equally considering working on contract or going back into a firm as an employee?*

For many people, the decision is taken from them. Someone

comes along while you are unemployed and offers to hire you for a time-defined contract. Without other immediate prospects for employment, it seems foolish not to take the contract.

The world of work has many more contractual opportunities available than ever before. The newer generation of people coming into the workplace seems more comfortable with this situation than the boomers and old-timers. For many, life becomes a stream of contracts. The film industry illustrates this very well. Everyone brought together to work on the project, a new movie, has a term-defined relationship to it. Once the movie is completed, they are unemployed once again, until hired to assist with another movie.

You should, however, settle this issue in your own mind. What is your true preference? Some people definitely do want to get into long-term employment and will even turn down lucrative contracts so that they can continue to search for what they want. The opposite is also true.

If you are clear on what you prefer, then even if you accept a contract or full employment out of necessity, you know what you really want long term, and when the opportunity arises you can make the switch.

10

THE STAGES OF LIFE

THE CHESS CLUB - A STORY

The Crescent Chess Club meets every week. For the past seven years there has been hardly any turnover. Ed Turner moved away and Farley Jacobs withdrew because he found he was having trouble remembering his moves. He still comes around some evenings and joins into the social part of the evening. He makes the coffee and puts out the cookies.

The Club's eight regulars represent a diverse cross-section of ages and stages. It's true that it is a men's club - not that women wouldn't be welcome - but no one has ever found a woman who likes to play chess.

Eric Enders, age 45, comes with his son, Warren, who just turned 20. Both Mel Munroe and Moji Vishnu are in their 60s. Barry Popoff is 27, and his friend from the neighbourhood who has also become a regular, Irving Washington, is in his early 30s.

Dennis Washanicky doesn't like people to know how old he is. He keeps very fit, dyes his hair, and the rumour is that he has had the odd tuck or two. But his high school friend Ernie Michaels, who is also in the Club, says Dennis is 55. Ernie is 54.

Chess is the common denominator. Everyone in the group has a passion for it. Eric regularly takes top honours. He wins most of the tournaments and also usually takes a top spot when they play with other clubs. But no one talks about Ernie's exceptional talent for chess; they prefer to live with the illusion that they are more or less of equal ability.

Usually, at the end of the evening they stay, have decaf or tea and talk about the developments of the day or week.

One night they talked about employment. In fact the subject had permeated the group earlier in the evening when Ernie announced that he just "got the axe – been early-retired." "Good package," he said. "Got to figure it out, but maybe I won't work any more – or maybe I will. But who's going to want an old dog like me?" At 54, Ernie felt his work life was coming to a close. Yet deep down, he also knew that his financial situation was not going to permit him to stop.

Young Warren started the discussion during coffee later that evening. "I'm going to be finishing up my degree in a couple of years and I don't ever plan to be in the situation you're in Ernie," he said. "I'm going to be self-employed one way or the other. No one will ever be in the position to tell me my job has ended. I'm only going to take on jobs that have an ending, whether it's in a month or six. The most I ever want to work in one job is maybe for a year."

Dennis, with a mid-50s mind-set, couldn't hold himself back. "You have no idea what you're going to be up against in the world of work. You'll soon see that steady, long-term employment is the only kind that pays off in the end. You need security, benefits, a pension plan and regular pay to live a decent life in this world. You'll be in total chaos all your life the way you're describing it."

"Sounds like bo..ring ... is your idea of the good life! That's not for me," shot back Warren.

Barry Popoff, at 27, was an I.T. professional and had moved around to various jobs in his short career. Now he was at Vanty Tech, where his job was to work with one of their clients on a new LAN installation. "Warren may not have it totally right, but the way I have lived my life since graduation five years ago, is right along what he's talking about. I never intended to move from job to job, contract to contract – but it's just happened that way. That's the way I'm needed out there. I'm not happy about benefits and pension, but some of the jobs have paid pretty well and I've got a start on retirement savings, and, through our profession, I've got some benefits. I think I'll just keep on doing it this way."

His 30-something friend Irving piped up. "I've got a steady job which it looks like I can keep for a long time – although you never know. But I'm not learning any more. I've learned all there is to learn. I envy the variety that Barry has, even though sometimes he's really anxious about where his next job will come from."

The 60-plus guys, Mel and Moji had been very quiet. Both were retired, living on adequate but limited incomes. Mel cleared his throat and seemed a little nervous about saying anything. He didn't really want to take sides, but felt a little compulsion to set the record straight. "The best thing for any of us is to stay the course. If you have a job, keep it as long as you can. There's too much uncertainty in life without creating even more upset by job-hopping. If you can, do the job, keep your nose clean, and stay as long as they'll let you. I did that for 40 years and look at me – I'm pensioned and can concentrate on my chess game!"

Moji didn't really agree. "I wish I was still working. But everyone disagrees with me when I say that maybe I should go back to work. My wife says to forget it and count my blessings. My barber says I should be happy to leave room for the younger generation. My sons are always asking me if I'm 'up to this, or that' as though they think I'm weakening day by day. Just talking to them makes me feel weaker."

Eric Enders, at 45, didn't know what to think of this question. He was a manager in a small manufacturing company. Mostly he was involved in marketing, and he also managed a small staff. He was also aware that his company was up for sale and hearing that Ernie had got the boot was quite unsettling to him. If he were fired, he would definitely need to get another job. Where would he go? He had heard that at 45 you're over the hill.

"You're too young to retire," Eric said to Ernie. "If I could predict what was going to happen to our company, I'd get you an interview there. But it's probably not a good idea right now. We'll probably be under some other company's name within the year."

Irving Washington, 33, with a young family, had his own small plumbing business. He had worked with the previous owner for 10 years and then had taken it over three years ago. He was still paying him out.

Irving had been listening to all these comments. "Well isn't this interesting," he said. "We are really seeing some of the differences of the generations right here in our little chess club. We all have to live with anxiety and stress about our jobs. It doesn't matter whether you have a secure job – which doesn't seem very secure any more, or work on contract, or like me — I'm only as good as my reputation - and my income depends on the phone ringing."

"We all have different attitudes and views, but somehow the world doesn't seem to much care what we think. Each of us has to look after himself. Get a job, get a contract, get a business – it doesn't seem to matter. The best we can do is understand each other and where we are coming from. There are probably going to be a lot fewer real long-term jobs, from what I read in the newspaper. So, maybe these young guys are going to have to just be smart and look after themselves through short jobs and contracts. I know some of you older guys think that this could be the end of work-life, as we have known it. And you don't like it.

"One thing is for sure – I hope – that none of this is going to interfere with our chess games. I like the idea that there is something in my life, that at least for a while, I can count on keeping going."

But Ernie, who had listened to all this, didn't find it particularly helpful. "I am out of work, you know, and I really do think I'm going to need to get work. If I die in a couple of years - I hope not – then I've got lots of finances, but if I live to be 92, like both my grandfathers, then I am not in good shape. So I'm hoping you guys will keep your ears open for any possibilities. Let me know. At this point I don't really care whether it's a full-time job or a short-term contract. I just want to get back in there again."

Just then, Farley Jacobs the coffee-making, forgetful, former player spoke up. "We gotta get outa here – they're going to want to lock up in about five minutes. I don't think I can come up with too many ideas for you Ernie. But I'll put my brain in gear and see what I can do. Good talk though. I think you're all saying something that's right about what's happening and what should happen. And let's all see what we can do for Ernie. This world is about as mixed up as my brain is – but, anyway, I'll be here next week and the coffee will be on."

OVER A LIFETIME

Each stage in life presents its own unique challenges. What is it like to be a job searcher at the different stages of life? Responses to work-life are very different.

The New Recruits

The new, or almost-new, recruit generally expects to start in a junior role. She feels like she could do a lot more. She is idealistic about how an organization should be run and thinks there is a long, unending road ahead of her. She is expecting to '"live a life"' as well as work for a living, and doesn't expect to stay with one organization a long time.

This group, born after 1966 and before 1980, are not as dedicated to work life as older groups, although they have much of the knowledge and skill to be successful. They are adept with the computer, and know a great deal about how the world works. They are not happy about what they see around them in the world in general, and feel that the people in their parents' generation have really screwed things up. They would prefer to do a job, rather than work hours, and would like to be in a flat organization where they can have as much influence on decision-making as anyone.

They anticipate having difficulty getting the kind of work they want and expect to work on a contractual basis, or in shorter-term employment situations. They expect to make it on their own with little long-term support from an organization.

They know that they must constantly be in the job market. They learn how to search for a job early on, and recognize this as an important life skill.

The Middle Group

People born after the Second World War and before 1967 - the boomers - form a huge part of the North American population. Their attitudes and views have been dominant now for many years. This has been a mixed-up time in the world. Family breakdown has been rampant. World communication has allowed for the development of universal values. Organizational chaos, with downsizing, merging, elimination of whole groups of employees, elimination of many jobs and professions, and growth of the entire technology infrastructure has played havoc with this group. Yet they have been expected to provide leadership in these difficult times.

Boomers have suffered the most from this chaos. They have lost their jobs, have had to retrain and learn how to job search after thinking they had lifetime employment. They have had to provide leadership to the very different group coming up behind them.

This group has had a tremendous influence on every aspect of life just by its size. Its attitudes still hold sway, and as the movers and shakers in the power elites, it still insists that the younger generation pay attention to what it believes is right about how organizations function, and even how to search for a job.

The Final Years

Those people born before 1948 are now at, or nearing, retirement. They have become somewhat jaded about organizations. They feel they have seen it all – mergers, downsizing, state-of-the-art technology, and flavour-of-the-month organizational improvement processes.   They struggle with technology and often have had enough of being in responsible jobs. They smile at the enthusiasm and naiveté of younger workers, and know that the end of their work-life is not too far off.

Being fired at this point in life is particularly stressful. Few people enjoy having the end of work dictated to them. When people do leave a stable employer at "retirement," many prefer to keep working.   Even in their 50s, 60s or 70s, some people are still on the job.   They may not work as many hours, but they are productive.

There is a quiet push on the part of younger people to get them to stop working.   There is discrimination against the older worker today.   But, as the Baby Boomers, the group born after 1945, come to retirement, the attitude towards employed older people will change.   They will be needed in the workplace because they are such a dominant group.   Their skills will still be needed and the social system will struggle to support so many of them. Keeping them working will ease the financial strain and keep their needed skills on the job.

IMPLICATIONS FOR JOB SEARCH

The age and stage of life we enjoy shapes our attitudes towards work. These views also determine how we approach a job search. Those people who are in the position to influence employment choices, are themselves influenced by their stage in life.   For example, organizational recruiters are influenced by their stage in life when it comes to recruiting for open positions.

An older person approaching a company made up of young people will have a struggle being received well, even though he may be better qualified than other applicants.   Occasionally, forward thinking "young" companies will hire an older person simply to get another point of view, or the experience and knowledge the person brings.

A young person trying to break into an organization made up of middle-aged and older people, will also experience discrimination. Capable young people are sometimes not considered because of attitudes they express that are typical of their group, but are felt to be out of step by the older leadership.

QUESTIONS AND ANSWERS

- *Where are the job opportunities for people in their 50s, 60s and 70s?*

They don't exist in large corporations that are often releasing and retiring people once they get into their early to mid- 50s. However, these same firms will sometimes hire older people in contract and consulting roles. The difference appears to be that they don't feel they are burdened down by the liabilities of having older people, but can still take advantage of their expertise on a contractual basis.

Older people can get jobs as consultants and contractors, doing the work that they have spend their working life honing. Some start businesses. Popular businesses for older people are in the hospitality area, for example, as owners of Bed and Breakfast businesses. Some join in with their children to set up small businesses. Speciality retail businesses are sometimes a choice, or some form of entrepreneurial work like carpentry, catering, or animal care.

There is an army of people who work in security jobs in their later years. This at least provides an income for people who may have only basic government pensions. Often the work is not very stimulating to the creative mind. Older people are also found increasingly working in stores and restaurants, because of the decreasing numbers of young people available for these jobs.

Older professional people find employment in special assignments carrying out studies, working on special task forces, and consulting. Some of these talented people earn incomes by writing articles for publication, or even books.

Of course, there are some who simply carry on in the workforce, full-time, in jobs they have held for years. They have the expertise, have not slowed down, have their health and enjoy being productive and being paid.

- *How do people just graduating from college chart a career course?*

The conventional wisdom is that those just graduating will have several, even many, careers in their lifetime. Preparing for a particular profession, in the honest belief of being in that profession until retirement, is likely no longer valid in most cases.

Young people should prepare well for their first career. They should have in mind that they will likely be moving on from it, and be continually thinking about what the next step will be. Will it be in the same profession, but in a different aspect? Will they move to something totally different? What are some other things that come to mind as possible career directions?

Those who are supporting and encouraging the young should also realize that the world is fast-paced and today's great career may be in disarray in a few years, if not non-existent. They should encourage an open approach on the part of the young and new graduates.

- *With advancing technology, are there going to be jobs to go around in the future?*

Jeremy Rifkin[8], author of "The End of Work," predicted several years ago that traditional work settings would be in decline. He thought that the efficiencies of technology would reduce the numbers of jobs and that determined efforts were needed to create new kinds of jobs, to reduce the hours of work and take other measures to ensure more people could be productive and earn a living.

His predictions have not been borne out yet, as in North America, at least, there is almost full employment, according to government statistics. However, these statistics may not be completely accurate, as many people are not recorded. These include people no longer on employment insurance but still unemployed, people who have "given up" in their efforts to get work, and people who are employed in menial jobs when they are qualified to do much more. The statistics don't include people with limited resources struggling to start small businesses and who are not yet making sufficient income through their fledgling businesses.

In some developing countries there have never been enough jobs to go around. Thirty to 50 percent, or more, of the population is unemployed in some countries. Advancing technology can only make things worse.

At the present time in North America, the people with the most assured employment prospects are those with a good education. These people will have good prospects as far as we can see into the future. The problem, world-wide, appears to be one of education. If people get good training they can do many more jobs and can see how to create new jobs.

The answer to the question of job availability – increase your chances by getting well-trained and educated.

---

[8] Rifkin, Jeremy. The End of Work: The Decline of the Global Labor Force and the Dawn of the Post-Market Era. G.P. Putnam's Sons, 1995. 350 pp.

- *Given the stage of a person's career, what should be left out of a resumé or included to increase chances of consideration?*

For older people, increase your chances for consideration by leaving out references to a long history of employment. Say you have had "many years of experience" rather than "30 years." Also, go back only 20 to 25 years in recording your work history. The work you did prior to that time has little relevance for what you are doing today.

For the younger person, increase your chances for consideration by recording the skills you have in the use of technology and in soft areas, such as working on a team. Don't just make the claim that you have these attributes, but indicate how you have used them. Employers are impressed by skills and accomplishments, and this will help you if your employment history is thin.

Whoever looks at your resumé wants to find reasons to eliminate it so that the number of people to be seen can be reduced to a small number. Go through your resumé with a fine-tooth comb. What could be used to rule you out? The length of your resumé might be one negative. Keep it short.

- *How will an older interviewer approach a younger applicant?*

We all approach interviews from our own point of view and values. A young person would do well to be aware of what an older interviewer is likely to be concerned about during the interview. Is it conservative clothing? Is it the language of the young that might be a turn-off for him or her? Is it being too familiar by using first names?

The older interviewer may be thinking, "this person I'm interviewing is the same age as my daughter! And I know what she's like!" It's very important for the young applicant to talk about taking responsibility, understanding accountability and about being willing to gradually climb the corporate ladder. These are all things that the older interviewer is likely to value.

• *How will a younger interviewer approach an older applicant?*

The 25-year-old interviewer may have a great conflict when interviewing people who are in their 50s. Young people do see older people as being inflexible, not very energetic, judgmental and not good with technology. They wonder how long they will be around. In the course of the interview, the young interviewer will be looking for evidence to confirm these prejudices.

The older applicant does not want to fall into this trap. Be aware of how a younger person is likely, even unconsciously, to view you. The stereotypes are there. Deliberately, through responses to questions, show that you are outside this mould. If nothing else, you will create some cognitive dissonance for the young interviewer who may come to see you as an exception.

11

HELPING FIRED PEOPLE

Note: If you are currently involved in a job search, you may wish to show this section to family and friends.

Those who are close to someone who has been released from employment can be helpful to him or her. But real influence is often not exerted in the ways we might expect.

There are wrong ways and right ways to help someone who has been released from employment. Here are some of them:

WRONG WAYS TO HELP

- *By giving advice.* Many people believe they can be most influential either by telling others what they need to know, or by instructing them about what they should do. This works in organizational settings, so why not in a one-on-one setting? Yet harassing a friend or relative with a long series of "why don'tchas" often alienates the very person you are trying to help. Constantly telling someone what to do to solve his or her problems eventually comes across as a lack of confidence in ability.

- *By making extraordinary demands.* This is an extension of advice giving. An opportunity searcher who repeatedly hears insistent demands that she try this or do that, will eventually feel that the problem at hand is beyond her ability to solve.

- *By browbeating.* This is often done in soft and subtle ways (though also in angry blustery ways). The message transmitted is that the released individual is personally to blame for the job loss.

- *By distancing.* This is a technique used by family members and other people close to the terminee to deny the reality of the event. It is never talked about. The illusion is maintained that everything is normal. The released person will cooperate because it keeps everybody off her back.

The wrong ways to help, outlined above, result from anxiety on the part of the other people affected by the job loss. Intentions may be good. They may feel out-of-control of the situation and want more input. One way of "helping" is to push, cajole and force the job searcher to take action. Unfortunately these tactics often have the opposite affect.

RIGHT WAYS TO HELP

There are no panaceas. Any attempt to help another person must be genuine and flow from the context of the other issues being dealt with by the family or in the friendship. Here are a few suggestions.

- *Listen without prejudging.* The released person wants to be heard, even if some of the concerns being expressed are hard to understand and may at times be expressed in highly emotional terms.

- *Answer and suggest only when asked.* In their hearts, most people know what they need and will ask for it. Wait for the question to be asked, then respond only from within the framework it provides. Don't use it as a springboard to consider all the faults of the other person. It is important above all to be truthful and direct within a context of positive regard.

- *Reverse roles.* Sometimes this can be done deliberately – a kind of game where the job searcher and a close friend or family member take each other's roles in order to discuss the situation. If done well, this can lead to greater self-understanding on both sides. If nothing else, it forces the helper to be in the job searcher's shoes and imagine what she is going through.

- *Provide practical help.* If you are a friend or family member, you may know someone you can call, on behalf of the job searcher, for introductory purposes. Only do this if specifically requested. Perhaps you can type or spell better, or make specific suggestions on the resume. You might be able to run an errand that will make things proceed smoothly. But you don't want to take so much initiative that you take it away from the job searcher. Providing very practical, hands-on assistance may be more meaningful and helpful than anything you could say. It provides concrete evidence that you care.

Much has been written about the "helping relationship." The main features of this relationship – the ones that are common to all the theories, and which seem to transcend time – are certain personal "ways of being there" for the person needing help. *In this connection, be genuine! Express personal warmth, and finally, demonstrate positive regard for the person in need of your support.*

QUESTIONS AND ANSWERS

- *Is there any advice when both partners are out of work?*

This situation provides an excellent opportunity to collaborate at a difficult time. All of life's options are open. The constraints of a job are gone. If the pair is also without a family, they are in the favorable position of considering moving to a new location, if that is desirable.

Each can support the other in job search efforts. If one has a talent for resumé preparation, he or she can help the other. They can shore each other up when the going gets tough. They can report to each other on the achievement of targets for calls, interviews and ad responding.

The situation can be viewed as an opportunity and should be!

- *To what extent do you bring the children into the picture when one parent is out of work?*

Children know. You can't hide the strain and anxiety of one parent being out of work. It is always better to bring them fully into the picture. If they are very young, they may need reassurance about basics such as getting fed. If they are older, discussions can be held about how they, the children, can interpret the situation to their friends, and at school.

- *How do you deal with the situation where one partner has faced the loss of his/her job on several occasions?*

This situation will become more the workforce norm as time goes by, and as more of us work for shorter periods of time within different organizations. As well as experiencing the hurt that comes from being released over and over again, consider the advantages of it. A person so affected becomes much more adaptable and can function in a greater variety of work situations. Also, he is more likely to have a larger number of opportunities to increase skill and experience levels, as a result of being in different work environments.

Take control of your career. Establish your next assignment as a time-limited contract. Knowing that it will end after a certain number of months or years allows you to begin to plan well in advance for the assignment after that. You have turned a negative situation that has been out of your control, into a positive one, kept within your control.

12

NEGOTIATING COMPENSATION

A job offer eventually comes to most active job searchers. Will you be ready to deal with it? As with the rest of the opportunity search, you don't want to act too quickly. No one expects an immediate "yes" to a job offer, although many people do just that. Drained by a long search or a lengthy period of unemployment, complimented by the offer, fearful of not getting any other offers, or at least not for a long time, the anxious applicant says yes – on the spot.

"May I have some time to think it over? I would like to discuss it with my spouse." Few organizations will refuse this request. Now you will have the time to make a considered response to the organization's first position on compensation.

Timing is a key factor in the negotiating process. Before you start talking about compensation you need to be sure the company really wants you. Watch for such signals as: they say they want you; they introduce you to others; they show you your possible workstation or office; then provide extensive information on how the company works. They clearly are going to offer you a job. Negotiations should begin only after you have reached this point.

QUESTIONS TO CONSIDER AFTER THE INITIAL JOB OFFER

• Is this THE job you want, or is it close enough to qualify?

• Have you checked out the company thoroughly – its management, long term prospects and financial viability? Will you and the company fit? Do you share enough of the same values?

• Do you know enough about the working conditions? What hours do they work? What attitude do they have towards working evenings and weekends? Do they have adequate benefits and insurance? How many weeks of vacation will you have? Do you have to travel far to your work location? Will the company pay for your relocation if a move is required?

There are many considerations and reasons to check out the organization in a careful and deliberate manner.

GENERAL PRINCIPLES OF NEGOTIATION[9]

If an organization has indicated they want you, they are usually prepared for the detailed discussion to arrive at a satisfactory arrangement. If they aren't willing to take the time to carefully discuss this important life decision with you, what does that tell you about them? In spite of indications of urgency, the

---

[9] Much of the material for this section has been drawn from workshop materials prepared by Dr. Edward E. Morler of Sonoma, California, a leading expert in the field of negotiations.

organization's representatives will take the time to negotiate, if they really want you.

Question them closely to find out what they hope to achieve by having you on staff. This is an important step because it sets the stage for an informed negotiation. You might find, for example, that their major criterion is to get someone in place quickly, and that salary is a secondary consideration. For this reason, you may also want to slow down the process to ensure that they know enough about you and you about them, to know that this is a good match.

Try to determine where they are really coming from. Start by analyzing the recruiter. What motivates this person? Is she hard-nosed on the issue of salary? Is she simply trying to follow company policy regarding position equity? Is the negotiator a creative problem-solver or someone who is content to get by in life? Your diagnosis of this person will give you clues as to how to negotiate for the job. With the creative problem-solver, you could suggest ways of changing the job to make it more valuable to the organization, fit your abilities better, and perhaps pay a higher salary. With a lock-step company person, your chances of coming up with creative and beneficial solutions may be very limited

Be prepared to continually show the organization the various ways in which you can be valuable to them even after they have made their initial offer. This will reinforce that the right decision has been made. Also, you want to put yourself into a stronger negotiating position based on your qualifications, experience and skill.

Know your compensation objective. What do you feel you are worth? To set an objective you need to do some research. Find out what people with your qualifications are being paid. You can ask friends and acquaintances. Look for objective data on what organizations are paying for your experience and qualifications. There are surveys and studies constantly being carried out by compensation consultants and by large organizations on this topic. Where would you place yourself on the salary grid? Look at your experience, your skill level, and what you have accomplished in the past. Take into account any special skill and talent that you bring to the table. Set a compensation objective that is realistic, in keeping with your qualifications and your chosen industry.

Know your personal bottom-line in terms of the lowest compensation you will accept. The bottom-line is usually the compensation that will keep you whole. You won't have to mortgage your house or take out a loan, or sell things in order to take the job. You decide in advance that pay below your bottom-line is unacceptable.

The gap between your objective and your personal bottom-line is your negotiating area.

Try to get the employer to make the first offer. This gives you an idea of their bottom line and will help you with your counter. You are in a much stronger bargaining position knowing their initial offer. Coupled with your diagnosis of the company and the person you are talking to, and your knowledge of norms in the industry, you now also have their starting position before you. You can make an informed judgement about the level of salary and the range of other benefits you should seek.

The person you are negotiating with may not be the final decision-maker, and may have to take your offer back to a more senior person. The negotiator may be able to negotiate up to a certain level. If you persuade her that you deserve more, she may have to go back to her superior to get approval.

If they agree to more salary and other benefits, they may expect you to change your expectations in some way. It could take a good turn from your point of view. They may come back to you saying that they will pay you more, but expect you to take a higher level of responsibility.

In advance, **identify the range of other items** you would like to discuss with them. See the next page for a listing.

Don't negotiate for items fixed by company policy unless you know that the company sometimes deviates from its policies. For example, a leased car may kick in at a certain level of employment. If you are seeking a lower position, it may be a waste of energy to negotiate for this benefit.

Negotiate for the future. For example, if the salary level is lower than you would like, negotiate for a potential or automatic raise, at the three or six-month review time, provided performance has been satisfactory. Many managers don't want to exceed a certain company agreed initial salary, but are willing to negotiate for a future benefit. At that later point, they will have the authority to approve a raise based on performance.

As you negotiate and compromise your initial position, if possible, **get something in return for each increment of compensation you give up.** For example, for a reduction in salary, you might get the agreement of the company to provide you with a state-of-the-art computer to use at home, linked to the company's network. Negotiators often expect that there will be trade-offs. If you simply drop your price, they assume it was only a position anyway, and had no bearing on what you really think you are worth. If you ask for another benefit, or consideration, then you convey that you really do feel worth the initial level, but understand that the salary might not be possible for a variety of reasons. You indicate that this can be made up in other ways.

Your final objective is to negotiate a win-win outcome. You want the organization to feel that the solution is a good one. If they go away feeling they have been conned by an expert negotiator, this may come back to haunt you another day.

Be conscious of using good interpersonal skills when you negotiate for a job. If the company representative becomes annoyed at you because of the way you are presenting yourself, or speculates that your interpersonal skills are not up to standard, you may find the negotiations coming to a grinding halt, with you on the outside, and you may not have a satisfactory explanation as to why.

WHAT IS NEGOTIABLE?

- Salary
- Vacation
- Car allowance, leased car or transit pass
- Fitness fees
- Conference and course attendance
- Professional organization fees
- Stock options
- Salary increments, performance bonus, profit sharing, signing bonus
- Severance upon termination
- Parking expenses, a parking spot, transit pass
- Business expense allowance
- Moving expenses, all or partial; subsidy on discounted sale of home
- Housing loans or second mortgages
- Housing allowance for jobs in remote areas
- Cellular phone for personal and business use
- Computer for home use, personal Internet connection
- Clothing allowance
- Day care allowance

SOME FINAL ADVICE

Compensation negotiations can result in obvious differences because of far-apart views and value systems. If the two sides mutually reach a point where neither will budge any further, this usually signals that the negotiation is complete. You will either accept the last offer of the organization, or walk from the table.

Advice on what **NOT** to do:

- Don't put yourself down or go out of your way to express your limitations. At the same time, be honest about areas of experience you don't have and things you can't do.

- As mentioned earlier in this chapter, don't feel you necessarily have to conclude the negotiation in one session. There are occasions when this is appropriate. But it is not unusual to meet the organization's representatives several times before completing the negotiations.

- Don't be naïve about the negotiating ability of the organization's representative. They have experience, while you negotiate on a matter as important as your job only once in awhile.

QUESTIONS AND ANSWERS

- *How do you respond when the search firm you are dealing with is insisting on knowing your previous salary?*

You may have to give them some indication of where you were, or are presently. They are presenting candidates to the organization, and don't want to put forward people that the organization discovers it can't negotiate with, possibly because of too-high salary expectations. When you tell them your previous salary, make it clear that you had other elements of compensation that aren't included (if it's true). You might also indicate (if it's true) that you don't feel the job you are applying to is comparable to the job you are leaving. In other words you don't want to be locked in to your previous salary level.

- *How do you deal with "what are your salary expectations," early in the interviewing process?*

You can directly ask that this question be left until later, until you know and understand the expectations of the job and the interviewer has a better feel for your capabilities. Most organizations will respect this request.

- *How do you know when you are beginning to step over the mark and your negotiating is beginning to be annoying?*

You may have an indication if you find the organization's interviewers are beginning to distance themselves from you, after giving you strong indications that the job was likely yours. Also, by being inconsistent you could annoy the interviewer. For example, you may state a salary expectation one day, and then you come back asking for more. You are likely to cause yourself problems if you hold firm to the point of stubbornness seemingly for no purpose. Be prepared to walk from the negotiation if you don't feel you can live with the compensation that appears to be the final offer. Otherwise, accept the offer.

- *Can you negotiate when you are starting in your first or a very junior position?*

You can't negotiate as much. But that does not rule out bargaining altogether for the imaginative beginning employee. You can suggest a future review of your job and your salary. You might want to see if you can get agreement for consideration for the paying of fees for courses, after you have been with the organization for a year or two.

* *What do you do when you are told, early on, that the offer is the only and final offer?*

In a nice way you might say, "no matter what I come up with, or add to the discussion, there is nothing else to talk about?" This will likely elicit a response of "it depends." Thus, the door opens for further negotiation.

* *How do you believably negotiate when you are desperate for a job?*

The person who has been out of work for many months without any opportunities often feels desperation. More than ever, you should carry out a full negotiation. The organization will have a greater respect for you as a future employee if they feel that they arrived at a fair agreement with you. If you simply accepted the first offer, they would wonder why? Are you truly desperate? Are you really a more junior person and thus the offered salary was too high?

Take your time to get the organization to the position of really wanting you. Stay away from the topic of compensation until the indications are there, that they believe you are their solution. Then have a full and fair discussion of all elements of compensation.

13

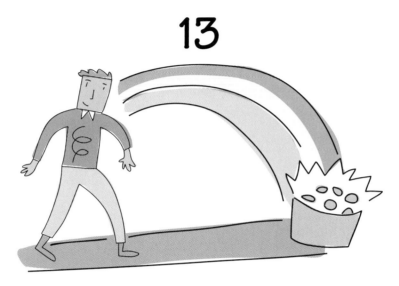

A CAREER STRATEGY FOR LIFE

When it comes to careers, most people don't plan systematically. Perhaps in some cases it's not really necessary. Many young people follow in the footsteps of their parents and successfully pursue a career in medicine, law, education, finance or agriculture. Some people get offered opportunities in line with their interests and abilities, and without much conscious thought pursue a constructive and interesting (for them) work life.

Increasing numbers of people, however, continue in career areas where they are unhappy and unfulfilled. Many find themselves downsized or released from an organization that not only does not need them, but also does not need any people like them. Their base skills have become redundant.

INSIDE AND OUTSIDE

Strategizing about one's career is becoming more important. Today there are fewer people in stable work settings pursuing work they like. The transitory nature of work and work settings leaves many people frustrated and unhappy, and in need of a plan.

We have suggested a planning approach; consider who you are and what career you should pursue. To successfully plan, you need to consider where you have been, your education, experience, accomplishments and skills. Coupled with this you should systematically look at interests. You would not happily pursue a hobby that doesn't interest you. Your work must not only use talents that you have or can acquire, but must also engage your enthusiasm.

All of us, particularly today, feel the stress of the uncertainty of work and the anxiety of others around us. How much of this angst can we stand? Knowing yourself and your ability to absorb all the hurts, slights and pain of living is also important in strategizing about your future.

These are all "inside you" considerations. Outside of you, out of your control, changes take place. Areas of employment decline, while others come on-stream. You may be affected. Organizations "streamline'" their workforce constantly, which usually means fewer employees are needed, thanks to efficiencies created by technology. More people are out of work.

You must plan what you want to do, and match this with the reality of the workplace. A career plan can help in the immediate situation, and can also provide a way of viewing the future. Usually the strategy will be to have several options in mind because change, out of your control, may wipe out a preferred direction or two.

SOME FINAL ADVICE

Be ready for change.

Keep your resumé updated. Be aware of changes in the workplace. Keep in contact with people through continual networking. Know how to respond to questions about your skills and experience.

Don't rule out any possibilities. People pursue advanced education at all stages of life. New careers are started by people in their 60s. Some people intersperse overseas assignments into their stream of life work. Entrepreneurial aspirants try out their dream. Many people are taking roles in the new economy of electronic communications and business.

Be kind to yourself.

We play our part on the "stage of life" for only a few years. No one has been able to defeat the end of life, nor many of the difficult diseases that precede the inevitable. We want and need to live beyond our work life. Most of us want the fulfilment of family and community life. Pursuing interests and hobbies brings us happiness. We want to contemplate the mysteries of life, to consider our lasting contributions, and to contribute to improving the lives of those who are struggling.

Our career strategy should not leave out living and giving in its broadest sense.

Related Readings

Alberta Advanced Education and Career Development. **Occupational Profiles**. Development and Marketing Branch of Alberta Advanced Education and Career Development, 1996.

Bardwick, Judy. **Danger in the Comfort Zone**. AMACON, 1995.

Bardwick, Judy. **The Plateauing Trap**. AMACON, 1986.

Bolles, Richard C. **What Color is Your Parachute 2001**. Ten Speed Press, 2000.

Bower, Sharon Anthony and Gordon H. Bower. **Asserting Yourself**. Addison-Wesley Publishing Company, Inc., 1991.

Bridges, William. **JobShift**. Addison-Wessley Publishing Company, Inc., 1994.

Csikszentmihalyi, Mihaly. **Flow: The Psychology of Optimal Experience**. Harper Perennial, 1991.

Dudley, George W. and Shannon L. Goodson. **The Psychology of Call Reluctance**. Behavioral Sciences Research Press, Inc., 1986.

Dudley, George W., Shannon L. Goodson with Dr. David K. Barnett. **Earning What You're Worth**. Behavioral Sciences Research Press, Inc., 1995.

Dunckel, Jacqueline. **Business Etiquette Today**. International Self-Counsel Press, Ltd., 1987.

Dychtwald, Ken. **Age Power**. Penquin Putnam Inc. New York, 1999. 266 pp.

EdITS. **Career Occupational Preference System**. 1982.

Employment and Immigration Canada. **National Occupational Classification**. Canada Communication Group – Publishing, 1993.

Foot, David K. **Boom Bust & Echo**. Macfarlane Walter & Ross, Toronto, 1996. 245 pp.

Garth Toombs & Associates Inc. **The Career Planning Workbook**. An unpublished copyrighted workbook, 1996.

Goldberg, Beverley. **Age Works**. The Free Press, New York, 2000, 230 pp.

Jeffers, Susan. **Feel the Fear and Do It Anyway**. Ballantine Books, 1987.

Kolbe, Kathy. **The Conative Connection**. Addison-Wesley Publishing Company, Inc., 1990.

McNally, David. **Even Eagles Need a Push**. Delacorte Press, 1990.

Morler, Edward E. **Negotiations**. A copyrighted course workbook, 1993.

Moses, Barbara. **Career Intelligence**. Stoddard Books, Toronto, 1997. 283 pp.

Moses, Barbara. **The Good News About Careers**. Stoddard Books, Toronto, 1999. 226 pp.

Pitcher, Patricia. **Artists, Craftsmen and Technocrats**. Stoddart Publishing Limited, 1995.

Shechtman, Morris R. **Working Without a Net**. Prentice Hall Inc., 1994.

Strong, E.K. Jr., J.C. Hansen, D.B. Campbell. **Strong Interest Inventory**. Consulting Psychologists Press, Inc., 1985.

NOTES

NOTES

NOTES